D0545559

Tales from the Public Access

A Celebration of Lake Life
in the Land of Ten Thousand Lakes

Linda Marie

Tales from the Public Access
A Celebration of Lake Life in the Land of Ten Thousand Lakes

ISBN 978-0-9827175-1-6

Cover Art by Brenda Olson, www.brendaolsonart.com

Printed in the United States of America.

OnTheLakePress
Clearwater, Minnesota
www.onthelakepress.com

Dedicated to Ken,
who shares morning coffee,
afternoon happy hours,
and the public access
with me.

Acknowledgments

This book would not have happened without all the lake-loving folks who provided me with lake stories. So thank you, whoever, wherever you are.

Providing priceless encouragement, support and critique were my Clearwater Writers Group—Eve Wallinga, Jerry Hoem, Pat Nelson, Char Hopela, Mary Schenten and Judy Kallestad; my St. Cloud writer friends—Bob Roscoe, Jeanette Clancy, Bill Morgan and Marilyn Brinkman; and my fine-tooth-comb reviewer—Denise Kantor. Thanks to all of you!

A book just isn't the same without a cover and Brenda Olson came through with the artwork for this one. Thanks, Brenda!

And finally, thanks to my biggest supporter—my hubby Ken—for proposing the idea of *Tales from the Public Access*, for taking on the task of in-house technical support, for filling in photographic gaps, for providing invaluable editorial comment, and for sharing with me so many memories from our lakeside deck.

Preface

After years of writing essays based on my own life experiences—published in *Another Angle: Reflections on the Ordinary*—I pumped out three novels, which currently reside under my desk, gathering dust.

Once I completed the third one, I pondered what writing venture to next focus on. "Please," my husband pleaded, "not another novel!"

I have to admit, writing a novel is all-consuming. Probably best if one doesn't have a full-time job, a husband, children, family, friends, or—in semi-retirement years, which is where we are now—a deck! Like the one from which we so enjoy our morning coffee and afternoon happy hour.

That's where we were when my husband suggested I go back to writing essays. "Because you're so good at it," he said. *Gotta love that guy.*

Reflecting back on my newspaper reporting days, when I was involved in the community and all its doings, I had been privileged to meet new and interesting people and to discover amazing endeavors every day. The best part was, not only did I get to "report" on a particular event, I always had my own corner of the paper to post my own thoughts. And I had thoughts!

Virtually falling out of my head—faster than I could write them all down.

As we spent yet another happy hour on the deck, which happens to be just eight feet from one of our Land of Ten Thousand Lakes lakes, I answered my husband.

"But my world is smaller now," I said. "I don't have exposure to big-life goings-on anymore."

At that moment, we happened to be watching a boat being launched at the public access—a mere 50 yards away. Easily within earshot, we listened to the boat full of life-jacketed young kids eager to begin their lake adventure. As the launcher tended to parking his truck and trailer, the kids began wailing as the boat sunk to the bottom of the shallow water just off shore.

You guessed it. No plug. We heard the disappointed kids continue wailing as the waterlogged boat was pulled out of the lake and down the road away from the anticipated summer fun.

My husband turned to me. "Why don't you write *Tales from the Public Access*?"

We had already been verbally sharing stories of kids' antics out on the swimming raft, the thrill of neighbors meeting in the middle of the lake for Fourth of July fireworks, stars reflecting in a calm lake on a moonless night, and endless loon and other wildlife phenomena we had been experiencing right here from our lakeside deck

I started writing.

The result? Twenty-eight tales typical of any one of Minnesota's ten thousand lakes.

Prologue:
Theatre de la Public Access

You wouldn't think that here on one of the tiniest bodies of water in the center of the Land of Ten Thousand Lakes we would have our own theatre. But we do. And the only cost for an extraordinary performance is a practiced awareness of nature happenings around the lake.

We call them *Lake Shows* and there is no shortage of them here at *Theatre de la Public Access*.

Fin Shows

The first show I remember seeing I called the *Fish Show*. I was just about to walk out the door to drive 60 miles to work via I-94 when a splash on the lake caught my eye. I moved closer to the window and saw another splash. And then another.

Still early in the morning, the wind hadn't yet come up to ruffle the glass-like surface of the lake. The calm water made it easy to see hundreds of long, sleek fish randomly jumping up out of the water and splashing back in.

Such a mesmerizing display, even after 20 years of fish shows, makes it hard to leave home—especially to go to work in the big-city world of concrete.

Later that first year, during the hottest part of the summer, the weeds were so thick on the lagoon side of our house, I couldn't even throw a line in for a crappie or a sunnie without it getting tangled. That's when I was introduced to the *Carp Show*.

These mammoth finned creatures entertained me—for as long as I could stand being outdoors in the heat—by twisting up and out of the throes of water lily tangles and then flipping and flopping back in.

After repeat performances all these years, we haven't a clue why they do this. Oxygen needs? Reproduction patterns? Or, perhaps, the tasty worms and insect larvae found on lily pads are just irresistible . . .

We often see carp hunters on the lake side of the house in watercraft designed especially for spearing the humongous fish. While we watch the hunters balancing with their spears or bows on a railed platform built up on an ordinary fishing boat—camouflagely painted of course—we can't help but think, *If they only knew what show was playing in the lagoon.*

Feathered Friends Shows

One of my first springs here, I took a day off from driving that 120-mile round trip and treated myself to a day at my word processor. That's it—just a word processor. Not a PC. Not anything online. Just one step up from a typewriter—though larger than one of the first microwaves. Some of you may remember.

I sat at the too-high hand-me-down desk from my grandmother—on a too-high ergonomically incorrect stool—and relished taking time to key in a story on the contraption that provided a tiny bit of internal memory. Then, after clicking the print key and inserting one sheet of paper at a time, I'd have a printed version of my insightful words. If I thought my words were insightful enough to keep, I'd save it all to—what was it—a 3.5" floppy? Though it wasn't really floppy at all. I never understood that.

As I paused while thinking of my next astounding sentence, a movement outside the window directly over my word processing machine caught my attention. And there I caught my first *Goose Show*. Waddling between my cabin and the next was a parade of geese. Several families of geese—each with 5, 6 or 7 babies.

I had noticed them, for a few weeks by then, parading through the lagoon behind the house, around the end of the peninsula and out into the lake on the front side. I had never seen them march from the lagoon to the lake between the cabins.

But on this day, that's exactly what they did. And, maintaining their family order, they waddled back into the water and paddled on. While this shortcut made sense to me, I never again saw them do that.

On another day, right around that first *Goose Show,* I was preparing to again hit I-94, when I decided I needed to first wash the dirty dishes heaped on the kitchen counter. The back door next to the sink already open, I welcomed the spring air coming through the screen. I set down my purse, lunch and extra wrap, and tended to domestic business.

I made a point of not clanking the dishes too much, in order to hear what might be going on outdoors. Sure enough, I soon heard a squawk I had never heard before. Without stopping to rinse or dry my soap-dripping hands, I quietly turned off the tap and looked out.

There, only a few feet the other side of the screen door was a pileated woodpecker. Except for the Woody Woodpecker cartoon character—complete with a head of wild red hair and an oversized yellow beak akin to Daffy Duck's—I had never seen one.

This bird, its huge claws desperately trying to keep its 18-inch-long body hanging on to the suet I had hung from a tree months before, pecked away at the high-fat seed-imbedded treat in spite of my open-mouthed awe. It did not look like a cartoon character at all. Its zebra-striped head, neck and long, narrow beak were topped with a distinctive well-cropped red crest. The stripes continued down its throat, eventually melting into its oversized all-black body—rather than "Woody's" blue tuxedo, white-gloved character.

That was my first *Woodpecker Show*. Though this is now a regular occurrence, I still often wonder what I might be missing when I leave home.

Weather Shows

Before moving here, eight feet from the edge of a lake—which seems to put us closer to weather for some reason—I never noticed the differences in rain.

For instance, before the first *Shower Show* I experienced, I didn't know that rain drops came in various sizes. When I saw drops on the lakeside window between us and the marigolds on the deck, I learned that a spring rain is soft. Generally not even requiring closing the patio door, we can barely see the zillions of tiny, close-together drops sprinkling the lake.

If we didn't see the drops gathering on the window, we wouldn't even know it was raining.

A *Hail Show,* however, is another story. In spite of potential damage to roofs and cars throughout the neighborhood, watching the tiny ice balls make foot-high splashes in the lake beats any television show.

We don't watch a lot of TV—don't have to when we have the *Theatre de la Public Access* right out our door. Besides, the satellite signal goes out at the first breeze of a storm, so most of the time we just watch what's going on outside our windows.

At the first sign of a *Thunderstorm Show,* while others are gathering flashlights and snacks and going to the nice carpeted lower level of their split levels, we have not yet been enticed to go to our own.

Our "lower level" is only accessible by opening hinged lattice work on the outside of the house, climbing over a three-foot high wall, crouch-walking under the width of the deck, securing a trap door open until we gingerly low-crawl through it to the shallow dirt-floored, spider infested—and who knows what else— claustrophobic crawl space, and close the heavy door behind us.

Not real appealing. So, instead, we just watch an oncoming thunderstorm from the comfort of our living room.

Though maybe we should be worried and take precautions, watching the amazing changes in the weather makes us forget about everything else. Well, unless my mother calls to tell us we should be worried.

But at each change of color in the sky or the clouds, or the onset of thunder, lightning and lake waters being blown clear across to the other shore, we cannot bring ourselves to turn away from the *Thunderstorm Show.*

In the event of a post-thunderstorm rainbow—or two—which we like to call a *Double Feature,* my hubby and I can't resist inviting neighbors, living the newly required 200 feet away from the lake, down to our lakeshore to join us for the multicolored wonderment of a *Rainbow Show.*

Night Shows

While Minnesota heat and humidity can be suffocating, we have put off installing air conditioning because we don't want any mechanical humming muffling the sounds of nature, especially the nighttime ones.

First in the spring to woo us to sleep is the *Frog Show.* Though my naturalist hubby can identify which particular amphibian is actually doing its thing, I can easily enjoy the harmony of the individual croaks, peeps and trills without knowing who's doing what. Like classical music, the frog chorus can put me right to sleep.

And then there's the *Cricket Show.* While crickets might be singing all season, the *Frog Show* must drown them out during the earlier part of the *Night Show* season, as I hear the crickets mostly toward the end of summer.

The *Cricket Show* reminds me of summer nights in my open-windowed bedroom in the big city where I grew up. Because the only window was at the foot of my bed, I slept with my head in the foot area to better hear the chirping as it lulled me to sleep. While the city didn't have all the nature noises we have here, cricket cricks are nostalgic and still comforting to me.

The only *Night Show* that can beat the *Frog Show* or the *Cricket Show* is the *Star Show. Star Shows* are noiseless, but captivating. Have you ever been at the edge of a calm lake on a moonless, cloudless night? If not, you are missing out on one of my favorite lake shows.

Believe it or not, if you look out over a dark calm lake, reflections of stars will shine back at you. While next-to-impossible to describe the magnificence of such a sight, I can promise that you would be amazed, too. And watching one of those stars fall out of the sky and into the lake with its reflection following leaves us breathless with awe. We almost expect to see a splash.

Our neighbors, not able to experience this from 200 feet away from the lake, are somewhat disbelieving when I tell them about the amazing *Star Show*.

~~~

When we sometimes think our little lake home isn't big enough for the two of us and our too-many hobbies or occasional overnight company, we also know we cannot give up our front-row *Lake Show* seats at the *Theatre de la Public Access*.

Table of Contents

Ice-Out

"Yup, the ice will be out early this year." I looked at my husband toasting the frozen lake with his coffee cup.

The sun had barely peeked out from between scattered puffs of clouds on this early March morning when he insisted on taking our coffee to the deck. So there we were, in winter jackets, hats and gloves, side by side in not-yet-warm plastic deck chairs, mostly warming our hands on the cups rather than drinking the coffee.

"You said that last year," I said, watching my breath drift away.

He ignored me. He does every year.

~~~

Ice-out.

This Land of Ten Thousand Lakes phenomenon makes gamblers out of the most straitlaced. Neighborhood gatherings produce green stuff changing hands and challenges over when every last hunk of ice will be melted. Or the earliest-ever date. Or the latest-ever date. Even after the fact, it seems to be debatable.

I got up, retreated to the house, came out with a blanket and tucked it around my lap as I settled back in the plastic deck chair we hadn't used since before the lake iced up. The temp had just inched up over the freezing mark, never mind that last week it barely hit zero. But it promised to be a sunny day and that's all it took to get our hopes up. I took a swallow of coffee, as we watched a car drive from the public access out to the middle of the lake where its occupants set up their fishing gear.

My husband slumped a little. And sighed.

We finished our coffee, simultaneously got up and went inside. With still-gloved, chill-induced shaky hands, he poured us both a fresh cup and took his to his office. I took my cup and chilly body and headed for the bubble tub.

It's been a long winter.

~~~

By the end of the week, after several days of sunshine and temps hovering around 40, we had our first glimpse of water at the edge of the lake. Being a rare windless March day, a pre-ice-out celebration was in order, which meant happy hour would take place on the deck.

It was glorious. Sunshine on our faces, our bottoms on warm chairs and a cool glass of Chardonnay in fairly toasty fingers, we watched fishermen walk, rather than drive, out onto the lake with their gear. "Yup," Hubby said, "any day now." I refilled our glasses. And then we watched the sliver of open water widen. Slightly.

~~~

The next week brought snow, sleet and rain. My hubby was beside himself as he peered through the patio door glass at the darkening lake. "This'll make it go quick," he said.

"Want a taste?" I asked, holding a spoon up over the pot of bouillabaisse I had been stirring. After a few housebound days, we had reverted to warm, cozy winter activities—cooking and eating. No response. I tasted it myself. "It's only the middle of March."

~~~

When the precipitation abated, a week and three meals of the saffron-laced seafood chowder later, temps reverted back to below zero. Way below zero. For days. We listened to the thunderous cracks, characteristic of the big freeze at the beginning of the winter season, echo across the lake and end in quakes under our house. In addition to its usual eeriness, it was disorienting to hear those freezing noises during the wrong season.

While we generally enjoy listening to the antics of the lake, my hubby was devastated at the ice-out setback. The strip of open water just beyond the deck had again frozen over. When 40-mile-an-hour gusts prompted windchills to dip into the minus-30 range, he was flabbergasted. "How can this be happening?" he asked.

"Do you remember . . ." I started. He was looking out the window, watching our plastic chairs dance from one end of the deck to the other. ". . . the year we first met and I invited you out for a walk on the lake about this time of year?" He hears this story every year at just about this time. "It was our third date." No response. "And the windchills were just about like this?" Nothing. "And we couldn't even go for our walk?" I waited. "And, remember, we had to find something else to do for the whole afternoon?"

It worked. He turned toward me, a devilish look in his eye, and grinned. It works every year.

~~~

Finally, at the beginning of the third week in March, temps went from a high of 10 to well into the 50s practically overnight. As open water quickly extended several feet out from shore, we started hearing noises from the bowels of the lake we had never heard before. Unlike the big freeze thunderous cracking sounds, these quick-thaw cracks were almost like a gunshot attached to a spring, which traveled across the lake with a "broingggg yoing yoing yoing yoing yoing ..." By the time the "yoings" reached the open water in front of the deck, they dissolved into waves, which lapped onto shore.

"Won't be long now," Hubby said. During the next few days, only the snow completely disappeared, but we were hopeful. He scratched "suet" off the grocery list attached to the fridge when he saw a female bluebird extracting treats from the eaves of the garage. "Time for the birds to eat bugs."

Not intending to dissipate his current bliss, I reminded him that we weren't yet up to the annual high school state basketball tournaments. And everyone in the Land of Ten Thousand Lakes knows what happens when busloads of teenagers are on the road heading into the Twin Cities from all corners of the state.

Luckily, this year, only rain, wind, fog, and what Minnesotans call "snow showers" plagued tournament travels. *Maybe he's right. Maybe it "won't be long now."*

~~~

When the sun came back out a few days later, my hubby took the cover off the pontoon, still on blocks in the backyard. I said nothing. Even when the rain, wind, fog and snow showers returned—for days on end—I said nothing. When temps dropped enough so that the snow began accumulating, I said nothing. Hubby wrote "suet" on the grocery list.

While we land-dwellers dealt with rain, wind, fog and snow— in any combination—the wood ducks flew over and kept on flying, evidently looking for more than that mediocre stretch of open water at the edge of our lake. The nest box, so lovingly crafted and recently cleaned out by my hubby for their return stood neglected.

~~~

Finally, during the last week of March, sunshine and warmer temps brought us outdoors in just our shirt sleeves. We went for walks on our winter-dirty road, smelled spring in the air and said hello to neighbors we hadn't seen in months, which allowed for updated ice-out predictions. We made a little fire in the pit at the edge of the lake at sunset. *Is spring finally happening?*

While we watched more wood ducks fly over in their quest for the perfect new "home," we heard the unmistakable warble of loons. Looking up, we relished the sight of them returning to our lake and watched as they circled, looking for a place to land. We looked hopefully at the open water on our shoreline, not adequate even for the wood ducks. The loons must have thought the same, as after one more circle, they went on their way. *Spring. Wishful thinking.*

~~~

I awoke the next morning to an empty house. After pouring myself a cup of coffee from the already-made pot on the counter, I looked out the window toward the lake. What open lake there was sported near-whitecaps from a fierce west wind. The resulting sparkles from the sun teasing the caps was a photo op in the making and gave me an inkling as to what my hubby might be up to.

Checking the corner of his office where he keeps his longest lens confirmed it. Knowing he'd be a while trying to capture a potential wood duck or perhaps a hooded merganzer—loons at this point were out of the question—I scoured the bookshelves in anticipation of an indoors day.

Two hours later, thermal cup empty and Canon memory full, he came in to warm up. "Maybe," he said, "I'll catch them during their afternoon jaunt." Not able to feel the bitter wind inside the house, we enjoyed the abundance of sunshine coming through the windows, making it easier to pretend spring might actually soon happen.

Late afternoon, when the sun was perfect to catch the glint in a duck's eye, he was back at his photo post. As the house began to cool down, I curled up in my rocker near the gas fireplace with Sandra Brown's latest release, glad I'm not the wildlife photographer in the house.

After a couple of hours, he came back in, warmed his hands over the fireplace for a few minutes and announced he was going to check the forecast for the next few days. I went back to my book.

Eventually, I heard from the back hallway, "Need anything from the store, Hon?"

I was in the middle of one of Sandra's romance scenes. "Nope," I said, turning the page.

When he returned an hour and three sex scenes later, I forced myself to put the book down and move away from the cozy warmth of the fire to see what was important enough to make him run into town. He doesn't often need to run to town for anything—well, besides suet. I peeked in the bags he had set on the kitchen table.

One bag contained salmon fillets, jumbo shrimp and—lo and behold—crab legs. I looked up at him. "The legs," he said, removing his jacket. "On sale."

Another bag contained an assortment of fresh veggies. "Asparagus?" I asked.

"Well, it's spring somewhere."

The next bag held five rental movies. *No wonder he was gone so long.*

The last bag—enough wine for a week. I tipped my head at him in question.

"It's not gonna be spring here for a while," he said.

~~~

Sure enough, the next day we were snowed in. And the next. Though it just happened to be April Fools' Day and seemingly a cruel joke played on us, we toasted Mother Nature with crab legs and Chardonnay.

By the time the groceries, wine and movies had been exhausted, we were back on the deck checking on the ice-out progress. The previously thawed strip was covered with a new thin coat of ice. When the sun peeked out, we heard the soft crystal-like, bubble-popping melting sounds that were music to our ears.

"Yup, it's gonna happen," he said. "Any day now."

I reminded him that ice-out, in the last 20 years, had happened during the first week in April only once. "We might have a couple weeks to go."

I hated to see him get his hopes up, but he wasn't going to let me burst his bubble. Instead, he went around back and cleaned the snow off the pontoon seats. I decided to go indoors and see what Sandra was up to.

~~~

Temperatures warmed up during the next week and just when the sun came out enough to beckon us back outdoors, another round of 40-mile-an-hour winds sent the patio chairs down to the other end of the deck as if to say, "Not yet."

"This wind," Hubby said, "will take this ice right out."

I have to admit, high winds do help, but the ice was still thick enough that it would take 80-mile-an-hour winds to "take this ice right out." I hated to think where all that ice might end up.

The wood ducks didn't care about the wind and finally claimed the wooden box intended for them as a home. This made for a happy hubby. By the third week in April, the snow had all melted and there was enough open water to assure us that ice-out just might happen—some day.

My hubby put the suet feeders away.

Linda Marie

Three pairs of geese—here to stay—cruised the shoreline looking for nesting spots. Trumpeter swans graced us with their presence by an overnight stop on their way farther north for the summer. A great blue heron swooped down and landed nearby. We heard sandhill cranes from the swamp across the road.

I checked my flower garden for signs of crocuses. All right, I know that was premature, but I get my hopes up, too, you know.

By this time, happy hour on the deck was a given. In spite of the still-half-frozen lake, we were content to hang out on the deck, our faces turned up to the April sun, which in April felt as good as a July sun. The loons finally found enough room for a landing and a pair settled in, giving my hubby and his camera plenty of photo ops as they fed and frolicked in the shallow waters near us.

~~~

Into the fourth week of April, I thought about the wagers made around the lake, spanning the entire month of April, as to the date of ice-out. Though I hadn't had a specific date in mind, if pushed, I would have bet money on the second week of the month. My hubby was sticking to his "any day now" prediction.

Then, one sunshiny afternoon during happy hour on the deck, watching—what else—the lake melt, we closed our eyes to the sun's rays, savoring the warmth on our faces, listening to the red-winged blackbirds and wishing our wine glasses would be magically filled without us getting up.

Magic happened, all right, while our eyes were closed, which didn't involve a glass with a stem. We opened our eyes to an ice-free lake.

~~~

And who won the wager?
When it comes to ice-out, everyone wins.

Linda Marie

Saffron Seafood Bouillabaisse

Cook 6 minutes or until tender:
1 T olive oil
1 clove minced garlic
¼ C. chopped onion
¼ C. chopped celery
¼ C. diced carrot
¼ C. chopped green pepper
¼ C. chopped red pepper
salt & pepper

Add & cook 10-15 min. until potatoes are tender:
2 14.5 oz cans diced tomatoes & juice
¼ C. mushrooms
¼ C. zucchini
juice from 2 6.5-oz. cans chopped clams (reserve clams)
½ lb. chunked potatoes
¼ t. cayenne
1 bay leaf
1 t. crushed saffron soaked at least ½ hour in ¼ C. white wine

Add and simmer 15 minutes:
¼ lb. scallops
¼ lb. crabmeat
¼ lb. mussels
¼ lb. shrimp
¼ lb. shucked oysters
several baby lobster tails
¼ C. dry vermouth or white wine

Stir in gently:
2 cans reserved chopped clams
1/8 C. chopped parsley
Serve with crusty French bread.
Serves 6-8

∽

For the Birds

Q uiet and calm.
That's what the public access is here on the lake during the off-season. Quiet and calm. No matter the weather, just a few weeks before the calendar decides it's spring, my hubby and I are looking forward to maneuvering the pontoon back up the rutted gravel road leading to the access and back into the lake where it belongs.

Actually, we are not exactly looking forward to the maneuvering part but, rather, the toodling part once it's in the lake.

We relish small signs reassuring us that spring might just eventually happen.

Fish houses, by law, are by now off the lake, while snowmobilers—with or without a law—aren't venturing out on the mushy ice. As for us, we are too chicken to even walk around the edges of the semi-frozen lake anymore.

Mounds of snow deposited in the parking area of the access are just beginning to melt, resulting in puddles and mud. Lots of mud. Children don't even need to be told to stay out of the mess. And when just the right breeze carries the earthy aroma of the meltdown to our deck, we almost believe spring will happen.

So, yes, it's quiet and calm here this time of year—lakeside. Quiet and calm is not the story in our backyard.

When I moved here almost twenty years ago from the big-city life to this little cabin, the deck—a mere eight feet off the lake—was an indescribable treat. Needless to say, that's where I spent most my free time, soaking up the sunshine and as much clean country air as I could. It wasn't long before I started noticing a variety of birds hanging around without any invitation from me.

First to appear in this Minnesota spring were robins. I watched the orange-breasted wonders gorge themselves on earthworms from the wet sliver of yard between the lake and the deck. In fact, at that time, robins may have been the only bird I could confidently identify. We had them even in the city. Worms, too.

When I caught a glimpse of something unidentifiably orange, I immediately added "bird book" to the shopping list affixed to the fridge. The next week, upon the advice of my new Audubon resource, I nailed or-anges to the railing of my deck. Voilà! Baltimore orioles.

When a neighbor suggested topping the orange with a spoonful of grape jelly, I was in for another fine-feathered thrill. Back in the house, a glance out a window made me think I was imagining the tiny flying creature—clearly not an oriole—

heading straight for the sweetened orange. Rather than landing, it hovered, wings just a blur in their movement to stay airborne.

Bird book in hand, I inched open the door to the deck and tiptoed outdoors to get a better look. While leaning forward a bit to better see the tininess of the hovering being, I heard a hum behind me and barely had time to duck before being dive-bombed by a similar tininess. I backed into the house and opened up the book.

A trip to Walmart was in order.

Once the newly purchased bright red feeder was filled with sugar water, according to its accompanying instructions, I headed for the door opening from my kitchen onto the deck. Reaching down for the handle, I thought about the red shirt I was still wearing. *Hmmm.* I looked at the red feeder in my hand, the orange and purple oriole feeder on the deck and back at my shirt. *Not a good idea.*

A few minutes later, sporting my most-faded gray T-shirt, I again tiptoed out the door, holding the tempting red feast at arm's length. The hummers were ready and waiting. Wishing I were wearing an arm-length glove like the ones wild exotic bird trainers wear, I quickly hung the feeder on the hook I had already prepared, backed up and plopped down in one of the deck chairs. The show began. I had no clue dozens of tiny hummingbirds had been hiding out just waiting for attention. I was in hum heaven.

A flash of yellow the next week led me to discover goldfinches and thistle seed, resulting in another Walmart run.

Before the end of that first year in my little country cabin at the edge of the lake, the public access a short swim off my shore, I took stock of my life. I was barely forty. Life was good. I kept an eye on mysterious activities at the access during the not-so-quiet-and-calm season and, in this, the quiet and calm season, I was watching birds . . .

Watching birds? I found myself wondering what I would do when I was old.

~~~

Fast forward twenty years. I'm still watching birds. I didn't know twenty years ago that it wouldn't get boring, that I wouldn't be cheating myself out of other old-age activities. Not that sixty is old age, but when I was forty, I might have thought so. At any rate, I'm not planning on getting bored with bird watching any time soon. Not in another twenty years or another twenty after that. And, best of all, I now have someone to share the sport with.

I don't know if it was me or the potential of an ultimate bird habitat that lured my hubby-to-be to hang out here with me. With only the lakeside feathered fliers I could claim to have lured to my deck as regular visitors, he must have seen something in my rather dreary backyard I didn't.

Now, thanks to my bird-loving hubby, it is plush with gorgeous dogwoods—red branches a visual pleasure against the snow in the winter and berry-laden through the other three seasons—inviting a variety of songbirds and, of course, good ol' robins. Other berry bushes—elder, winter, snow and choke— nestled in here and there, assure enough for all our winged guests.

Thinking of fruity yogurt, blended smoothies, ice cream toppings and hand-picked treats for the grandchildren, we planted and babied raspberry and blueberry bushes for years before finally being rewarded with fruit. Alas, the plump juicy berries, without fail, vanish before daybreak the day after I see the not-quite-ripe berries and think "one more day." And if I were ever inclined to make crabapple jelly, I'd have to beat the cedar waxwings to the tree.

The heated birdbath my hubby religiously keeps clean, warm and filled with fresh water attracts birds we didn't know might be in the area, even if only for a day or two. The first time we saw half a dozen bluebirds frolicking in the frost-rimmed bath, we wondered if our vision was deceiving us.

With the window of my office facing our backyard bird habitat, I look forward to sharing my first pre-dawn cup of coffee with the earliest winged risers. Sure enough, before it's light enough to see colors, the shape of the cardinals' puffed up bodies and unique crests silhouetted against the dimness of the rising sun gives them away.

Round two—as soon as it's light out—will bring ravenous blue jays. The three pair of them this year attack all the feeders and any other bird that might dare to enter their breakfast territory.

While woodpeckers of all shapes and sizes get their fill of suet from feeders my hubby keeps full, we're feeling fortunate we don't have a wooden house. Flickers, nuthatches, chickadees and brown creepers, too, eat their share and I have no doubt the local butcher will soon be able to retire off of us.

Every once in a while, when we think we've seen them all, we'll catch a glimpse of a species once again requiring the well-worn bird book. Scarlet tanagers, indigo buntings, rose-breasted grosbeaks . . . This year it was pine siskins and red-polls—hundreds of them at a time descending upon us like leaves blowing in the wind.

Now, toward the end of the lake's quiet and calm season, while my hubby is still trying to attract as many birds as he can, I am wondering what effect heaps of discarded seeds and hulls might have on my lilies, in the event summer does make an appearance. Hopefully, the ground-grazing juncos will clean them up for me.

The pine-cone lard-based bird treats I made and hung out are starting to melt and drip. My hubby says it's time for birds to search out nature's own treats.

Soon the red-winged black-birds' twittering will be letting us know that spring has indeed arrived. Tree swallows will be making a show of catching flying insects to feed to the teeny beaks vying for attention from the multitude of nest boxes attached to the garage. And we'll be watching. For many years to come.

Quiet and calm?

Not so . . . for the birds . . .

Pine Cone Winter Bird Treats

Combine 1 lb. just-barely-melted Armour Lard
with 4 cups of a mixture including any of the following:

bird seed
nuts
seeds
berries
grated carrot
raisins
oats
cracker, bread or muffin crumbs
cereal
Use your imagination!

Let mixture cool & thicken enough to spread.
Spread mixture onto pine cones, the bigger the better.
Using fish line or string,
attach an ornament hanger to top of cone.
For extra bird appeal, attach a string of cranberries
and for the holiday season, a red curly ribbon.
Hang anywhere outdoors where you can watch the fun!

Fishing Required?

ishing: *Required activity for those living on any one of
Minnesota's ten thousand lakes.*

When I moved to the edge of one of those lakes almost
twenty years ago, I wasn't sure just exactly how living in the
country would work for me. I had no experience with a propane
gas tank that had to be regularly filled in order to fuel my furnace,
let alone a buried holding tank, serving as my sewer system,
which had to be regularly emptied. Neither had been a factor in
the Twin Cities where I spent most of my life, so I also wondered
how these country necessities would affect my finances. I started
thinking about where I could cut costs if my "unknowns" had a
negative impact on my pocketbook.

It didn't take long for me to notice buckets of fish being
hauled away from various spots on the lake—spots I could almost
reach out and touch from my own shoreline. Remembering how
I'd enjoyed fishing with an old cane pole at Grandpa's lake when

I was a kid, it dawned on me that catching a few fish here and there could have a positive impact on my grocery bill.

A trip to Walmart provided me with a new cane pole—now available in three easy-to-assemble sections—bobbers, hooks and sinkers. I was proud of myself for remembering sinkers, a result of Grandpa making us take care of our own fishing equipment. He also made us put our own worms on the hook and take our own fish off.

Once home, I found a shovel in the garage—compliments of the previous owner of my new home and about the same vintage as my grandpa's—and set out to find me some worms.

Digging in a patch of warm damp dirt behind the garage brought me back to long, lazy, humid summer days with Grandpa on another of Minnesota's ten thousand lakes. In fact, I half-expected to see old coffee grounds mixed in with the dirt and worms, like I remembered from those good ol' days. I made a mental note to research raising worms. Keeping myself in the nostalgic mode, I rummaged in my recycling bin for a green beans can to put my worms in. Though cans these days don't rust like the ones I remembered, it satisfied the memories in my mind.

I took my green beans can of worms out to the edge of the lake, threaded one of the poor ribbed creatures on my hook just like Grandpa taught me, and threw the line in. While waiting for the bobber to bob, I looked the short distance across the lake at the line of fishers on the shoreline near the public access. In between my own bobber checks, I watched them throw  their lines out and immediately reel them back in—even though they hadn't caught a fish—and then throw them out and reel them back in, and then throw them out and reel them back in . . . *Guess fishin' has changed since I was a kid.* Though fishing techniques might have changed in the last 50 years, I was sure I could still tell a sunnie from a crappie and looked forward to that first catch, not to mention that first meal of fresh-caught sunnies. I mentally went over the ingredients for tartar sauce, hoping I had them all in the fridge. It didn't take long before the bobber bobbed, giving me reason to pull up on my cane pole—no reelin' required—and swing the gilled monster onto shore. *What's this reelin' business all about?*

I grabbed the line just above the hooked fish and held it up. I was sure it wasn't a sunnie. Anyone who doesn't know a sunnie when they see it certainly didn't grow up in Minnesota. And I was pretty sure it wasn't a crappie. But I seriously didn't have a clue what was attached to the hook at the end of my line. Straight to the phone I went.

"Dad?"

Naturally, he asked for a description.

"Fins," I said, "and scales."

And, naturally, he wanted more.

"Big," I added.

"Big what?"

"Big body," I said, "and, um, big mouth."

From my description and Dad's fish expertise—hey, he's been a Minnesotan longer than I have and, besides, he grew up with Grandpa—he surmised my first-caught fish at my new home was a largemouth bass.

"Now what?" I asked. Dad said he'd be right over to show me how to clean it. *Eeeuw. Forgot about that part.* He arrived half an hour later, armed with a really long, narrow, bladed device that he called a fillet knife.

"Fillet?" I asked. "Like taking the bones out? I don't remember Grandpa taking the bones out. Only the . . . um . . . the other stuff."

"These days," Dad said, "we take out both the bones and . . . um . . . the guts."

Eeeuw.

~~~

Dad proceeded to do whatever needed doing on one half of my dinner, complete with a detailed explanation of each task. As I expected, he handed me the knife so I could do the other half. I remember every disgusting detail of what I did to my half of the fish. And I remember Dad leaving me his knife for the next catch. I don't remember eating *this* catch.

I guess I had become accustomed to buying my seafood in nice neat cellophaned packages from the grocery store. Clean white flesh. No bones. No scales. No blood. No guts. Not even a hint of an undigested worm caught halfway down a fish's throat before its demise. Then I wondered if fish have throats.

My desire for skimping on the grocery bill in this fashion dissolved.

~~~

Fast forward a decade, which included a new hubby. Influenced again by witnessing buckets of fish pulled from our lake by outsiders and imagining the crispy-on-the-outside, flakey-on-the-inside tender fillets that would end up on their dinner tables, we decided to take action. And I was hoping I had caught myself my own personal fish cleaner.

Sure enough, first time out with the rods and reels that came with the new hubby, after I first impressed him with my worm-harvesting skills, we immediately caught two sunfish. Though we were thrilled to catch two sunnies right off the bat, we were not thrilled that they were too small to keep and less thrilled yet when we discovered they had swallowed the evidently too-small hooks.

Though he might have known more about fishing than I did, his expertise came from his own childhood summers on the rivers running through the eastern part of the continent. While assessing the situation, he relayed to me his bobberless, dough-balls-for-bait memories. I guess fishing for catfish on Chesapeake Bay wasn't quite the same as fishing on North Center Lake with Grandpa. After some thought, we realized that if we ripped the hooks out, the fish would die anyway, so we were obligated to keep them. And, gulp, to clean and eat them.

By the time my hubby remembered how to clean our meager dinner, it was late, the mosquitoes had made dinner out of us and we were tired. We debated having the energy to cook them—or not—but neither of us could remember how to freeze them. In water? In salt? In water and salt? Neither? Thus, we cooked up our few bites of fish and ate them.

That was the last time we went fishing that year—in fact, for several years.

With good intentions, we purchased fishing licenses each year but never got around to using them. Until this year. We decided that this year, being recently retired in the Land of Ten Thousand Lakes, we were probably required to fish.

It was one of those rare sunny April days when Minnesotans first believe that summer might actually happen. We had been watching the bucket brigade at the access for days, our mouths watering, imagining their crispy, deep-fried, decadent sunfish dinners. When we saw them starting to pull in crappies, we decided to go that route, which meant minnows for bait instead of worms. *Won't be the same.*

Instead of grabbing my trusty rusty shovel, a trip to one of the little bait stores we frequently passed on errand days was in order. While my hubby rounded up the fishing gear buried in the garage, I opted to make the minnow run. Stopping at the first bait shop I remembered seeing on regular errand runs, I didn't know what to expect, as anything I knew about bait required a shovel. I opened the door to the unexpected. I smelled it before I saw it—an oversized overly ugly mangy black dog baring its big crooked rotting brown teeth. Thinking I might be bait to this beast, I stopped breathing, let the door close and gingerly backed away.

At the next bait shop stop, I was greeted instead by a nice woman—not ugly, not stinky and sporting a nice white smile.

Whew! "Minnows," I responded to her inquiry. "I need minnows."

"What kind?" she asked.

Was this a trick question? Maybe she isn't so nice after all. "Crappies," I said. "We're going to fish for crappies."

I followed her to the back of the shop. "A scoop?" she asked. Seeing the blank look on my face, she scooped up a scoop of minnows to show me.

"Yup," I said, as if I knew all along. "A scoop. Exactly."

It didn't take long for me to blow my bait-expertise bluff— about as long as it took for her to dump the scoop of minnows into a plastic bag and knot the opening.

"How will they breathe in that bag?" "How long will they live in the lake?" "No warmer than how many degrees, did you say?"

Already smelling fish sizzling in the skillet, as soon as I arrived home, I managed to attach a wiggly minnow—trickier than a worm—to the larger-than-last-time hook and threw my line in the lake. I have to admit that I'd given in to the rod and reel thing. But, I would not—absolutely not—give up my bobber! In honor of Grandpa, of course.

Before I even had a chance to take a swig of my Gluek—

required Minnesota fishing accompaniment—my bobber didn't just bob, it disappeared. Shrieking enough to attract the attention of the whole line of access fishers, my hubby ran for the net I hadn't seen since the grandchildren played with it ten years before.

"Reel it in," he yelled. "Reel it in."

Everyone at the access had an arm in the air mimicking the reeling action. "Reel it in," they chorused. "Reel it in." Neighbors, lured out of their homes by the racket, joined us on the shore. "Reel it in. Reel it in."

I reeled. By the time my catch was in our holey, abused net, I wished the biggest, ugliest, stinkiest fish I had ever seen or smelled would escape through those holes. Alas, it had swallowed the hook and none of the curious onlookers dared to get close enough to remedy the situation. Actually, the biggest concern, after the ugly and stinky part, was identification of this finned fiend. Myself, I thought it might be a relative of the ugly, smelly four-legged beast that met me at the door of the bait shop.

Finally, it was determined to be a dogfish. *Guess I wasn't too far off.* A swift cut of the line eventually solved the swallowed-hook situation and freed us and the fish from each other.

It was a while before we thought about fishing again. Finally, nearing Memorial Day, we took our rods and reels back out. In lieu of a trip to the bait store, we opted for Grandpa's preferred bait, as an overnight downpour had left night crawlers in our yard begging for attention.

Standing amongst the red winter stems of barely budding dogwoods—much more pleasant than fish with a similar name— one of our first casts out that evening produced a huge, gorgeous sunfish. Proud of our catch, I remembered my neighbor from years ago, telling me he throws back the females during spawning season. I told my hubby this story and asked him if it was spawning season. He shrugged his shoulders as he turned the fish over a couple of times in his hand. He had his own question. "How do you know if they're female?"

Now, keep in mind, though my hubby is a scientist, a biologist and a medical engineer, none of this has anything to do with the reproductive life of a fish. Especially, a Minnesota fish. And I, being female and having lived through everything involved with the female reproductive system—from puberty through child-bearing through sex-ed talks with offspring and right into menopause—couldn't relate human anatomy to a fish.

"I'll call Crandall," I said. Everyone on this lake knows Crandall knows everything about fishing on this lake.

"Good idea," my hubby said as he put the ginormous sunnie into the ginormous bucket he had prepared for our ginormous catch.

Crandall's wife answered the phone. Crandall wasn't home, but after I told Mrs. Crandall what we wanted, she thought she might be able to help. "Well," she said, "it has something to do with an extra opening, um, somewhere, that, um . . . well, maybe Mr. Crandall better tell you. Tomorrow."

I relayed the message to my hubby. He threw our potential dinner back into the lake, packed up our rods and reels and made sure our bait was in a safe, survivable atmosphere. Me? I went into the house and took a package of store-bought tilapia out of the freezer.

An hour later, savoring the tender, flakey white fillets, coated with a cornmeal crust, lightly fried and topped with my homemade tartar sauce, we forgot about worms, a fish's reproductive system, and the tasks required of a fillet knife.

A few days after we learned which-opening-where is the decision-making factor in keeping a fish or not, we started thinking about giving the sport another shot. After all, we live on a Land of Ten Thousand Lakes lake. It's required! Isn't it?

We looked at the calendar for possible fishing opportunities. Monday night: dinner plans with neighbors. Tuesday: poker night with the guys. Wednesday: our usual dancing night out. Thursday: book club. Friday: lunch and movie with Mom. I always thought fishing was a good excuse to do nothing. Doing nothing sounded good. Back to the calendar. Saturday: happy hour with the girls. Sunday: visit the grandchildren. We came to the conclusion that we don't have time to "do nothing."

The next night, one of our enthusiastic fisher neighbors brought us a package of cleaned and filleted northern. We've never figured out if he really loves fishing or just likes doing nothing, but we are thinking that if we finally start catching our own fish, the accomplished fishers won't take pity on us and offer us their catches anymore.

Hmmm. Fishing required?

Linda Marie

Ken's Cornmeal Crusted White Fish

Start with any Minnesota-lake or supermarket-favorite
white fish fillets—thawed.

Prepare:
One paper plate of flour seasoned with salt & pepper
One shallow bowl of whisked egg
One paper plate of yellow cornmeal

Coat each piece of fish first in flour mixture, then in egg
& last in cornmeal and set aside.

Spray light amount of olive or canola oil on skillet and heat.

Cook each fish piece on medium heat, turning once until
lightly browned on both sides.

Serve with Lin's Tartar Sauce.

~~~

Lin's Tartar Sauce

Mix:
2 T mayo
2 T sweet pickle relish
1 chopped green onion or more to taste
1 T lemon juice
salt to taste

Oops!

One perfect spring weekend morning—perfect for coffee on the deck, perfect for throwing a line off the dock, perfect even for a quick jog around the lake. And that's exactly what one young man decided to do. The quick-jog thing.

As for us? We were content with the coffee-on-the-deck thing. On the quick jogger's third trip by the access, he took a quick detour into the bushes.

Oops!

We covered our eyes. Hmm, perhaps too much coffee before heading out?

Any visitor to the access, if they happen to glance around, cannot miss us on our deck if that's where we happen to be. Well, I guess that's where we usually are. But we are learning that not everyone expects—or maybe even cares—that they might have an audience. And it's not just joggers who are oblivious to their surroundings.

Nothing against peeing in the great wild outdoors . . . I'm pretty sure it's not against the law. Pretty sure . . .

Later in the season, during ideal swimming weather, we watched a couple of young teen gals whoopin' and hollerin' and laughin' as they ran down the access boat ramp and jumped into the water—over and over and over. It did our hearts good to see these girls having such good old-fashioned Minnesota lake fun. We settled in and enjoyed them while reminiscing of our own long-ago days of carefree innocent merriment.

But then one of the gals stepped just barely out of the water, not even trying to find any natural cover, shoved her swimsuit bottoms down, squatted and well . . . you know.

Oops!

Eyes again covered, we were somewhat relieved to think that, at least, maybe kids don't pee in the lake anymore.

On toward fall, early one morning as we were just beginning our coffee-on-the-deck thing before heading off to work, an elderly couple was in the process of launching their fishing boat. As always, we contemplated being able to soon enjoy such midweek retirement pleasures.

After a gulp of my coffee and a satisfied sigh, I almost choked at what we saw next. While the man waited in the boat, the woman made her way over to the bushes—her retired back side in our direct view—bent over and dropped her pants.

Oops!

Oh my.

I have a friend who recently moved here, to this Land of Ten Thousand Lakes little lake, after growing up in a big-city West Coast world of concrete far away from the outdoor nature we Minnesotans are accustomed to. Anxious to introduce her to our way of life, on another perfect spring morning I invited her for coffee on the deck, a great view of the lake and all its doings and, finally, a walk in the nearby woods.

When the coffee hit her, somewhere between the sheltering grove of evergreens and a thicket of prickly ash, I nonchalantly threw out her best option—Minnesota woods style—for relieving the situation.

"What?" she replied. "People really do that here?"

I rolled my eyes and summarized her three options. Home was too far away, so that left dropping her pants or wetting them.

She chose a secluded spot deep in that grove of pine trees and attempted the "dropping" option.

To no avail.

"I grew up on concrete," she explained, ducking under a branch on her way back to the trail. "I can't pee outdoors."

I again rolled my eyes as her third option prevailed.

Oops!

Now What?

A Minnesota May morning is like heaven on earth—and it's not lost on my husband and me. One Sunday morning, we settled on the deck with a second cup of coffee and marveled, once again, that in this Land of Ten Thousand Lakes, we have the good fortune of living a mere eight feet from the shore of one of them.

The trill of red-winged blackbirds, flitting about in nearby cattails, dared us to keep our winter feeders full a bit longer. A pair of loons, directly in front of us, preened and posed to the point we were sorry we hadn't thought to bring the Canon out. Sandhill cranes, though we couldn't see them, serenaded us from wherever they had chosen to nest this year.

Still in my pink and red flowered pajamas, a hummingbird dive-bombed me—a not-so-subtle request to replace the sunseed winter cardinal feeders with red nectar ones, please. Our faces turned upward, we felt the sun's warmth as it rose over the treetops to the left of our deck's southern exposure. Gazing lower at an old tree stump surrounded by the lake, which this year had been blessed with ample spring rainfall, we watched a painted turtle make its way to the stump's sunny top.

Leaves were silently bursting from willows, maples and oaks all around us. Crocuses had given way to daffodils, and tulips were right around the corner. Closed yellow water lily buds promised white-petal blossoms in the near future.

By our third cup of coffee, we had melted into the serenity of nature waking before our eyes. And then it happened.

The public access woke up.

Most of the multitude of lakes in this state have public water accesses, including a parking lot and boat landing, set aside for lake enthusiasts of all sorts. Ours just happens to be situated at a forty-five degree angle not far off the right side of our deck.

A "lake enthusiast" could be described in several ways. It could be a woman walking her dog taking a detour to enjoy the spring sunrise from the edge of the lake. It could be a couple of elderly men launching their Lund on an early summer morning with the idea of catching a sunfish breakfast. It could be a family needing a place to cool off in the August heat and humidity known only to Minnesotans. It could be autumn duck hunters putting in their floating camouflaged rig. It could be the bunch of bicycling adolescents from up the road stopping to skip rocks . . .

On this day, we looked over to find a 40-ish man with a truck full of kids backing his boat onto the ramp and into the lake. The boat was barely off the trailer when the kids—half a dozen at least—were out of the truck and jumping up and down at the shoreline, excited to get started on their lake excursion.

These days, when most families are choosing not to have six children, we speculated that this generous father perhaps allowed each of his three children to bring a friend. Our hearts warmed.

With the help of a dozen young arms and legs, several trips back and forth from the truck soon resulted in fishing poles, a bucket of bait, life jackets, beach towels and the required cooler of people refreshments neatly arranged in the boat. Finally, Dad settled five of the properly vested kids in the boat and unleashed it, handing its rope to the oldest of the bunch still on shore to keep the boat from drifting away while he parked the truck and trailer. He had hardly backed the trailer into an available space when he heard the same yelling we did. "Dad Dad! We're . . . Dad Dad! . . . sinking! Dad Dad! Daaaaaad . . ."

My hubby and I stole a quick knowing, familiar look at each other and settled in for the show. I wished I had a refill.

Dad immediately turned around and backed the trailer back to the shore. He jumped out of the truck yelling words we wished the kids wouldn't have had to hear, as they and the boat slowly sank lower in the shallow water.

Grabbing the rope from the handler on the beach, we could only imagine what Dad's hand, arm and now-undecipherable oral messages might mean. Actually, we weren't sure we really wanted to know. To the kids, it must have meant "get out of the boat NOW" because they all scrambled out, landing in the not-yet-warm water. The youngest two of the bunch rightfully wailed as the momentum of jumping out of the boat knocked them on their butts and sat them down into several inches of chilliness.

Handing the rope back to his first mate, Dad waded fully-clothed into the lake to the back of the waterlogged watercraft and shoved it toward the trailer. A few clipped superlatives designated a second mate to guide the bow toward the proper place on the trailer. A third mate didn't wait for an order—he was already at the crank designed to wind the rope up, thus guiding the boat up out of the water. When he couldn't budge it even an inch, a fourth mate joined him. The crank was big. The boat heavy.

Believe it or not, the coordinated efforts of this group—I'd like to think it was the coordinated efforts rather than the ear-splitting language—got the boat on the trailer. While Dad was catching his breath, his crew anxiously watched the lake run back out of the boat through the hole where the plug was supposed to be.

Once nearly empty, all eyes turned to Dad, like, "Now what?" While we couldn't hear what he said, we could imagine the words by the look on his face. The resulting looks on the kids' faces confirmed our thoughts. Finally, they all climbed quietly back into the truck and Dad drove them away, leaving drips of a spoiled lake day along the pavement.

Meanwhile, blackbirds trilled, loons preened, cranes sang and buds blossomed. The turtle stretched its head out of its shell, cocking it at us as if to ask, "Now what?"

Tiny 'Toon to the Rescue!

W e were hanging out on the deck the other day—I know, as usual—when a couple of guys pulled up to the public access and backed a pontoon down to the edge of the lake. This is not an unusual happening in early June but we watched anyway, of course, astonished at the size of the watercraft.

~~~

Over the years we have watched pontoons grow from no-frills, metal-fenced, two-seater vehicles, primarily used for fishing, to luxuriously cushioned, latrine-equipped, enter-tainment-centered barges large enough to house a family of four.

We reminisced of our search a few years earlier for a pontoon big enough for the two of us and maybe a couple of guests for an occasional toodle. And small enough that we could converse without yelling across 30 feet of plush carpet. It took us a long time, as most marine retailers don't even stock vehicles any less than 22 or so feet. Super-size doesn't apply to only fast food!

We remembered, too, one year when a house down the road had been sold and the new owners launched their boat—a double-decker, roaring-engine cabin cruiser complete with sleeping quarters. We doubted it had yet experienced a body of water smaller than Lake Minnetonka, which happens to measure more than 14,000 acres.

Our lake happens to measure a skimpy 49 acres. Hardly enough water surface to accommodate more than one skier at a time, let alone a two-story floating house. We wondered if they had even checked out the lake before deciding to buy their new home and put a second floating one on it. Only once did we see them or that particular ship. They must have moved on to larger waters.

We couldn't resist the urge to reaffirm our decision to purchase a tiny 'toon—a mere 15 feet long. Okay, so we did opt for "luxuriously cushioned" instead of two swiveling fishing seats but, at our age, we deserve a little comfort. And, I have to admit, I was imagining taking multiple neighbor friends on a 'toon ride. Believe it or not, I can treat six or seven girlfriends to a comfortable happy hour out on the lake, providing no one gains a hundred pounds or has to go potty.

~~~

"Cheers," my hubby said, holding out his wine glass. Well, it was happy hour, after all. And we were happy.

I held my glass up to meet his. "To us," I said as we clinked.

He brought his glass almost to his mouth to take a sip.

"Wait a sec," I said.

He froze.

"And to 'toons," I said.

We clinked.

"Oh," I said, "one more thing."

He again inched his glass back away from his lips.

"And to summer," I added.

Clink.

It had been a long winter. And a too-long, too-cool spring. Finally, sunshine on our pallid faces, thinking about discarding our sweatshirts, we were almost convinced that summer just might be in the cards.

My hubby held up his glass for one more toast. "Yes," he said, "to summer."

Clink.

~~~

Meanwhile, the two guys over at the access had easily—and surprisingly quietly—launched their pontoon. No yelling, no swearing . . . Not even as they stood on shore watching the 'toon calmly, silently drift away.

As much as we appreciate quiet, yelling comes in handy once in a while. Like, "You got the rope, Buddy?"

In this case, evidently, there was no rope to be had. I guess putting the vehicle in the lake just once a year doesn't lend to a down pat system.

I looked at my hubby. He looked at me. We looked back at the adrift vacant pontoon.

Aha! Tiny 'toon to the rescue!

After a couple of tiny tee-hees, Ken toodled over in the tiny 'toon, picked up one of the guys, toodled out to the titanic 'toon and deposited him on it.

All was well.

And then tiny 'toon headed off to save the rest of the world

Once Upon a Happy Hour

Once upon a time, near dusk on one of the first June days my hubby and I could enjoy happy hour on the deck without sweatshirts, we toasted the weather, the lake and each other.

We toasted the wonderfully welcome almost-summer fragrances surrounding us. We toasted flowering crab along the shoreline, lilacs in the neighbor's yard, basil in the pot just outside our kitchen door . . .

The lake was calm. The wind had died down enough to still the water and the leaves on the trees. After the last boat left the lake for the day, the access was quiet. Being midweek, the seasonal residents on either side of us were absent. Thus, the neighborhood was delightfully peaceful. Even the birds, usually our entertainment, seemed to have settled down early for the night.

Relishing the rare evening warmth, our serene solitude and the promise of summer to come, we were lifted out of our reverie by a hoarse chirping noise we didn't recognize.

"Blue heron?" my hubby mused. Looking in the direction of the sound, we wouldn't have missed the long-legged massive winged body of any one of the herons that regularly fish off the shores around us. No heron.

We heard it again. Hoarse, yes. Chirping, yes. We added bubbly to the description.

"Frogs?" I asked. Seeing as how we were smack in the midst of bullfrog season, we were satisfied with that deduction.

Until we heard it again.

"Too high-pitched," my hubby offered.

And again.

"And much too close," I whispered.

Without a word, we set our glasses down on the little plastic patio table between us, got up, tiptoed to the railing on the edge of the deck and cautiously peered over.

There, in the flower bed below, looking up at us, was a baby

raccoon. Afraid to move a muscle, we looked sideways at each other with only our eyes and then back down.

I couldn't resist capturing this moment. Slowly, quietly, I stepped backwards, slipped into the house, retrieved my camera and then tip-toed back out. We marveled at the raccoon's lack of fear as I snapped away.

"Curious little creature," my hubby whispered. And then he pointed. Lo and behold, coming right behind our little masked visitor were four more.

Now wishing we *did* have neighbors with whom to share this experience, we inched along the railing, watching as they inched along the flower bed all the way to the end of the deck. Fully expecting them to move on to the next yard, they surprised us by taking a turn and crawling up the stairs leading to our back door.

I immediately made my way to the top of the stairs and continued clicking as they struggled to get their short little legs up each step. My only lament, not thinking they would get so close to us, was that I had put the long lens on my camera. And here they were, only a few feet away!

My hubby had retrieved his own camera and positioned himself in the yard on the other side of the stairway. We looked at each other over the railing, muffling ourselves to keep from laughing out loud.

When the little critters reached the landing at the top of the stairs, I backed myself

into the corner and flat against the back door. I alternately held my breath and exchanged closed-mouthed chuckles with my hubby as we watched each one in turn frolicking, snooping and sniffing their way through a planter of marigolds and around my watering can.

Finally, with obvious apprehension, each somersaulted, akin to a new kitty, down the couple of deeper steps leading to the walkway.

We still stifled our laughter, although they seemed to care about us as much as kitties might have, as they meandered down the path from the deck and through our yard.

We couldn't bring ourselves to stop following them as they explored along the curved walkway, taking detours under the hostas, behind clematis-covered lattice work, around the ferns and over the decorative rocks in the gardens, on their way out to the gravel driveway. Then we just watched them mosey up the road, stopping to nibble on the neighbor's rose bushes and, finally, turning the corner and heading into parts unknown.

And that was happy hour on this once-upon-a-time day.

Happy Holiday!

Coffee hour started earlier than usual this morning. My hubby and I awoke shortly after sunrise to take our cups to the deck on this gorgeous clear blue-sky morning. The kind that promises to be a perfect Land of Ten Thousand Lakes lake day.

The lake was so still, we couldn't tell where the trees ended and their reflections started. We watched the loon chicks practice diving for breakfast before the adults shared their own catches. And, except for the baby cardinals and red-winged blackbirds vying for a place at the bird feeder, all was quiet.

As an extra bonus—this early in the morning—mosquitoes were nonexistent.

My hubby brushed the never-ending oak flowers off two of the deck chairs and we sat. Out of habit, we looked over at the public access. "Ah," he said, "it's still sleeping." He turned to face me and held up his cup. "Cheers."

"Cheers," I answered. We both knew it wouldn't be sleeping for long.

You see, today is the Fourth of July.

We figured we had about an hour before the lake got crazy. Thus, that would be the end of a peaceful coffee hour on the deck. We're a little spoiled. More often than not, we can count on quiet coffee mornings and equally quiet afternoon happy hours on our deck overlooking one of the smaller of the state's ten thousand lakes. But not on this day. Midway through our third cup, it happened. The access woke up.

By the end of that third cup, the three designated parking spots in this tiny lake's tiny access were occupied. A couple more vehicles with trailers were nosed into the trees along the no-parking edge of the area, several more parked between the no-parking signs along the road, and a line of watercraft-pulling vehicles were waiting for their turn to launch.

The thermometer on our southern-exposed deck had inched up over 80, heading easily up to the predicted 90. No sign of clouds. Still no wind. The only movement in the water came from the boats. My hubby took our cups in for a refill and came out instead with a Bloody Mary for each of us. With lots of ice. I didn't complain.

I felt like I was on vacation—when Bloody Marys on a summer morning are totally acceptable. You know, like the okay-ness of a Corona with your breakfast omelet in Cozumel. Similarly, on this day, as we forego our usual chores in lieu of watching the Fourth of July lake show, it seems anything goes.

When the first ski boat arrived—keep in mind that fishing boats are usually our morning visitors—we toasted each other with our breakfast drinks. "Happy holiday," he said.

"Happy holiday, Sweetheart."

While anything goes in the line of beverages on our deck on this day, anything also goes at the access. We lost track of how many vehicles and trailers were parked up the road behind the lush greenness of the trees this time of year. Probably better off if we don't know. Besides, we're more worried about what goes on *in* the lake once they've launched.

Before we reached the Gedney "Zingers" in the bottom of our glasses, we yearned to bring life jackets to the toddlers we saw not wearing them as they zoomed around the lake in a boat loaded with adults. We hoped the swirling tubers wouldn't swirl into each other or the paddleboats scattered here and there between the motorized watercraft. We crossed our fingers that the bikini-clad teens wouldn't fall off the bow of the boat during any one of its treacherous turns. We wondered if the skiers noticed all the docks and floating rafts scattered throughout the lake as they swooped out over the wake from one side to the other. And we cringed, too, at the unjacketed wildness of the jet skiers.

When we could no longer get a glimpse of the loon family, we decided to grill our Fourth of July kabobs in the lily garden— on the back side of the house where we couldn't see the lake. In lieu of tripling the shots in our drinks, we decided this would be an appropriate escape.

To the shaded, breezy side of the house we went. Sounds of lakeside craziness still surrounded us but were, at least, muffled. Throughout the afternoon, as the craziness accelerated at the same rate as the probable beer intake, we again crossed our fingers.

So, while we enjoyed the mass of multi-colored lilies growing over the holding tank in our backyard—as Erma Bombeck always said, things really do grow better in certain places—and the smell of lemony, herbed shrimp promised the perfect holiday feast, you may be wondering why we don't have our own company on the Fourth.

While we are fortunate to be able to enjoy the lake all year around, neighbors all around us are seasonal. Thus, our little neighborhood, on certain summer weekends, turns into the land of ten thousand tents. Living a mere few feet from a Minnesota lake, most days are holidays for us, but we save our own family get-togethers for another weekend. See? We're not totally anti-social.

And to prove it, as the lake calmed down later in the afternoon, we participated in the annual Fourth of July boat parade.

Boats, pontoons, paddleboats and canoes all decorated in red, white and blue, joined together to celebrate the day, the lake and this exceptional state in this exceptional country.

As the nautical parade cruised around the outer edges of the lake, we saw the loon family in the center, as if knowing they were safe now to scrounge for dinner. *Whew! One more year they managed to survive this day.*

Finally, as dusk turned to dark, I debated going to bed or staying up much too late to watch the fireworks. The fireworks show here, as on many lakes, is the combined effort of various lake residents—seasonal *and* year-around. Tired as I was— nothing to do with the breakfast Bloody Mary—I couldn't resist. And, though we can see the show from our deck, we opted to take the paddleboat out to the middle of the lake to join all of our neighbors and ooh and aah together.

It was worth every mosquito bite.

Grilled Lemon Thyme Shrimp

Mix in quart size zip bag:
1 heaping T chopped fresh or 2 t. dried lemon thyme
(or 1 T fresh or 2 t. dried English thyme plus ½ t. lemon zest)
3 T lemon juice
1 T olive oil
1 t. freshly ground black pepper

Add:
1 lb raw shrimp, peeled & deveined

Refrigerate 1 hour, turning bag.

Skewer shrimp onto bamboo kabob sticks and
grill 'til cooked through (140°) but not overdone.

Serve with leafy garden greens, mixed with
shredded carrots, chopped fresh basil & chives,
tossed with balsamic vinegar & olive oil,
and topped with shredded Parmesan cheese.

Garnish with lemon wedges.

Serves 4

What the Frickin'?

On this first real-summer day, I had been working in my office, glad it is situated on the shady side of the house. I welcomed the cool breeze coming in through an open window.

Though the calendar had just flipped into July, summer temperatures had been slow to come. The resultant cooler-than-average lake made for a tranquil beginning to lake life as we know it. Except for the loons staking out their territory and an occasional fishing boat, life on the lake had been exceptionally quiet. Too quiet.

Then I heard a loud *thunk-crash* followed by, "What the frickin'?" The first "frickin'" of the season. Though this common slang word is not exactly music to my ears, in comparison to some of the others that regularly float over the water from the public access, it's fairly tolerable.

I grabbed the binoculars on my way to a lakeside window.

I recognized two scrawny adolescent brothers from down the road—shorts hanging low off hips that didn't include a place to hang pants on. The only way I could ever tell them apart was that the oldest sported blonde hair and the other Woody Woodpecker red. They couldn't have been even a year apart. After watching these two brothers, along with two more—one younger and one older—grow up, I had never met their parents, so wasn't sure where the red hair on only the one came from. They stood knee deep in the lake shaking their heads at an obviously homemade wooden platform sitting half in the water. And half out.

The "half out" half seemed to be the problem.

Although the contraption wasn't quite floating, I assumed by the four big rusty brown barrels under the sorta-square wooden top that it might have at least been intended to float.

The youngest of the four brothers, scrawniest of all, baggy plaid shorts barely covering his privates, tested the still-cold water with one toe in preparation for wading in to join the other two. He didn't make it up to his own closer-to the-ground knees before retreating to shore. He looked back at the water and then at the other boys before shaking his head and deciding peeing in the bushes was a more pleasurable option for the moment.

I watched his older brothers assess the situation. Evidently, when the raft slid off the trailer attached to the ATV parked at the edge of the water, one side landed hard on the cement boat landing. Thus, the loud *thunk-crash* and the resultant "what the frickin'?"

One of the barrels had been forced up through the platform, dislodging boards every which way. As the boys inspected the underside and wiggled a few loose boards, I imagined their disappointment. I also wondered where the oldest of the four brothers might be, as it certainly looked as if they could use help. At the same time, however, I silently applauded them—in this age of video gaming and social networking—for devoting the first weeks off from school to such a wholesome outdoors summer project.

I put the binoculars away, strolled out to the deck, pulled up a chair and sat, ready for the next chapter in this particular saga.

After some serious assessment and tentative testing—a few kicks and some board-wiggling—the two older boys seemed to deem their creation floatable. Though the whole contraption certainly wasn't square anymore—if it ever was—they shoved their labor of love the rest of the way into the water.

They continued pushing it farther out away from shore, eventually swimming while still guiding it. Pausing, they urged their younger brother, as he came out of the bushes, to catch up to them. He gingerly made it into the lake up to his thighs and, with his arms crossed over his chest, yelled, "The water's frickin' cold."

Red-top yelled back. "Just go all the way under."

The oldest added, "Fast!"

Now holding his arms straight out to either side from his torso, he dipped down a few inches. The plaid on his pants had just barely disappeared beneath the lake's surface before he shot back up. "It's too frickin' cold!" I turned my head away as his hands found a warmer place.

Checking the progress of the other two boys, I again wanted to applaud as they succeeded in getting the raft to a good swim spot. Within viewing and hearing distance from both the access and the final destination of the raft, I had a ringside seat to the activities. While they romped on and off their creation, splashing and laughing, the youngest boy paced back and forth in the shallow water, arms back across his chest.

The older boys kept telling their younger brother to go under the water—up to his neck—fast! Anyone who grew up around Minnesota lakes knows jumping in fast is the only way to deal with our short swimming season. As for me, the older I get, the longer I wait to jump in. The year before, it had been August. This year may be the same. I marveled at the exuberance of the young.

Finally, the plaid pants again disappeared beneath the surface of the water, this time along with torso and arms! But not for long. He quickly came back up, yelling, "Fr-fr-fr . . ." He put his hands back in his warm place. ". . . ickin' cold!"

"You have to stay under," I heard from the raft. "And keep moving!"

Eventually, he did what his older, wiser brothers advised and began swimming toward the raft. "Hey," he yelled after a few strokes, "it's warmer this way."

About the time I felt my nose had had enough sun for the day, I noticed the absent oldest brother I had wondered about had arrived on the scene and was watching the others from shore. His three younger brothers, not noticing the newcomer, continued frolicking on and off the raft.

Finally, one of the big barrels dislodged from its corner and floated away. That end of the raft immediately sunk low into the water. The boy on shore shoved his hands in the pockets of shorts that hung well on his more mature body—there was hope for the others—and shook his head as he walked back up the access and off down the road.

I touched my nose and wondered if I'd miss anything if I left my post for a hat. I stood.

The youngest of the three in the lake retrieved the wayward barrel and began kicking while guiding it toward shore. The other two worked on getting the rest of the raft back to the access, its one end dragging in the water, making it a bigger challenge than getting it in the lake to begin with.

I sat back down.

By the time the trio arrived on shore—dripping and shivering—big brother had returned, power screwdriver in hand. Without a word, he gave it to the oldest of the younger three and, with no offer to help, again shook his head. Blonde and red heads bent together, the two middle boys went straight to work, repositioning the barrel and screwing down the upended boards.

I remembered my own brothers—well before indoor electronic distractions—building go-carts and racing on the elementary school's empty summer playground. And, thanks to an abundance of kids on our city block, the one over-grown empty lot had been transformed into a maze of forts and tunnels and kept us occupied outdoors for hours on end. And though we didn't have a swim raft to bring to Lake Nokomis, we packed lunches and walked the two miles to the big-city public beach most days during the summer.

Back in the present, I wondered the stories these four brothers would be telling their children some day. I watched young plaid pants shiver and dig in his shorts, as he looked back and forth between the brothers attempting to right the raft.

And then I watched the most-likely most-capable of them all walk down the road and away.

What the . . .

∽

"I Saw You . . ."

Not long after moving into my little cabin on the shore of one of Minnesota's smallest lakes, I acquired a swimming raft. I had never thought of owning one, but a neighbor was moving, had decided it was more trouble to move the raft than to give it away and was looking for a taker. My hand went up.

My grandchildren were just beginning to venture beyond the small shallow space I worked much too hard at to keep clear of weeds. I welcomed this floating eight-by-eight outdoor-green-carpeted addition to my lake life. I retired my lake rake and relished that I didn't have to worry anymore what to do with heaps of wet, stinky, aquatic weeds.

As swimming rafts are a common feature on Minnesota lakes, there are rules for placing one out in the middle of boatland. I followed them. In addition to making sure it didn't hinder the regular routes of motorized watercraft, I applied reflectors and a personal identification number according to the permit I had obtained from the county.

Upon anchoring it out about thirty feet from the end of my dock, I looked forward to the next visit from my young swimmers. It didn't take long before my children, grandchildren and friends made good use of it. They were all happy to paddle the paddleboat through the now-overgrown weed area, tie it to the raft in weedless water and jump in. Between these

visits, it became a regular meeting place for me to share a beer, the sun and a few laughs with my adult neighborhood friends.

Because of the proximity of my home to the public access, the raft was not much farther from the access than from my dock. Little did I know it might be deemed a "public" raft. I shouldn't have been surprised when neighborhood adolescents also began using it to share the sun and a few laughs.

I enjoyed watching them enjoying such a simple healthy summer activity. In my fairly quiet life here alone, I appreciated the sound of splashes, squeals and hilarity. I relished the nostalgia it evoked in me of my own all-too-rare childhood opportunities to do the same. With the advent of computers and video games, it did my heart good to see that kids still appreciated the outdoors and good old-fashioned wholesome fun!

Then, one day, the neighborhood kids enjoyed a little more "fun" than the sun and a few laughs. I had become so accustomed to the gleeful sounds coming from the lake as I went about my indoor tasks, I didn't feel the need to check on them very often. Taking a break, a cold iced tea in hand on the way to the deck, I stopped dead just after I opened the patio door. Backing up, I set my glass on the kitchen table and grabbed the binoculars.

By the time I removed my trifocals and focused the 10x50 Nikon, the moment was gone and I wondered if I had just imagined such a scene. Shaking my head, I set down the binoculars, put my glasses back on and reached for my drink. Looking back toward the raft, I watched legs and arms in every which direction as all five kids—two pre-teen boys and three barely-teen girls—jumped back into the lake.

After the usual splashing and accompanying squeals, one by one, they paddled toward the ladder to climb up and start the whole routine all over again. By the time there were only two kids left in the water, my curiosity got the best of me. I set my glass on the table, again took off my eyeglasses and picked the binoculars back up.

Sure enough, Trish, well into puberty too young, began climbing up the ladder. Still on the bottom rung, she looked behind her at Bobby, with his not-yet-as-developed hormones, not paying any attention to her while waiting his turn. She reached back and pushed her bikini bottoms down.

Visions of the Coppertone baby came to me. Only, in this instance, the puppy didn't do it.

When Bobby finally reached the ladder and looked up to grab the next rung, Trish looked back at her bare bottom. Feigning surprise, as if the lake had a mind of its own, she flung her long wet blonde hair to the side and yelled, "Oops," before pulling the suit back up and finishing her trek to the top of the raft.

Bobby casually took his turn on the ladder, still oblivious to Trish's exhibition. Like I said, the boys were younger and, well, literally, just boys.

I set the binoculars down, put my glasses back on, took my drink to the deck and settled in.

For another hour, I kept an eye on the "wholesome" fun I was accustomed to viewing, alternated with the still-ignored bottoms-dropping. Finally, the kids swam back to the access where they had left their bicycles. After a few more laughs while drying off with towels retrieved from the handlebars of their bikes, three took off to the left of the access toward their homes. Bobby and Trish, living to the right of the access, turned the other direction.

A clearing between clumps of dogwoods along the lake's edge just happened to allow me a clear view of the road, not to mention that I was also within earshot.

Trish, having longer legs, was well ahead of Bobby as they made their way up the hill. She stood on her pedals and, while exaggerating pumping and swaying, turned her head and yelled back, "I saw you, Bobby! I saw you looking at my butt!"

Little did Trish know that I "saw," too.

Not *On Golden Pond*

My hubby and I were dining on the deck. Not unusual for us, but on this mid-July evening, we were sharing our seafood extravaganza with a neighborhood couple who had never experienced our culinary talents nor the serenity of dining so close to the lake we could almost see our reflections in the water.

The lake was calm. Temps perfect for dining outdoors. The setting sun cooperated by throwing a few fuchsia sparkles over our almost-reflections. Our background dinner music consisted of peepers serenading us from the swamp across the road and crickets harmonizing from grasses all around.

To top off the fine-lake-dining experience, this year's mama and papa loons had chosen the shallow waters, just beyond the deck railing and swarming with small fish, for this night's lesson in teaching their little one how to dive for dinner.

We were barely into the first course of our meal, when we were interrupted by a sound akin to a gunshot.

"Thwack!"

Scallop-stuffed mushrooms, dripping in butter laced with home-grown herbs, stalled halfway to our mouths.

And then we heard another.

"Thwack!"

And another . . .

Tempted to drop our forks and dive under the table, we listened to thwack after thwack after thwack.

Instead of putting something *into* our mouths, *out* of our mouths, simultaneously, came, "What the . . .?"

From past experience, the first place we look for the source of unusual sounds is—you got it—the public access.

We looked.

And there we saw the thwackers. Three of them. Bikes tossed to the side, the familiar neighborhood boys, their shirtless swim attire displaying their pre-pubescent state, were hitting rocks into the lake with metal baseball bats. Though irritating in the midst of a lakeside dinner, it's not the end of the world, right? Just boys blowing off a little steam, right?

Not.

Not when, within batting practice range, the loon family was trying to enjoy their own fish dinner.

~~~

Loons. When one thinks of the Land of Ten Thousand Lakes, the first thing that comes to mind is loons.

Common Loons. *Gavia immer*. As a matter of fact, the Minnesota state bird.

When I first moved from one of the state's largest metropolitan areas to the edge of one of those ten thousand

lakes, I discovered that the sound made famous by the *On Golden Pond* loons wasn't the only call they made. Most astounding were the wails and warbles waking me at 4 a.m. each day from ice-out to migration. I immediately labeled this phenomenon a "loon orgy." They were obviously having more fun than me.

Now, twenty years later, we are still enthralled by their noises in the night. And we don't want to lose them.

~~~

My hubby and I, self-proclaimed protectors of the loons, lost no time in alerting the thwackers to the possible outcome of their sport.

We avoided using some of the words on the tips of our tongues—where the buttery scallops were supposed to be—as we outlined to the boys the potential consequences of their actions.

To them or the loons? You don't want to know.

Suffice it to say, the youngsters immediately felt the need to hightail it home.

Though the thwackers were a new challenge, we are often lulled out of our peaceful lakeside existence by the relentless roar of jet skis tearing up the lake or Independence Day boaters boasting their independence just when the loon chicks are beginning to venture off their parents' backs . . . Well, don't get me started.

Okay, maybe we're a little over-protective. But, year after year, we are thrilled when a loon couple graces us with their appearance in the spring and, after some scouting, chooses our lake on which to spend the season and, hopefully, raise a family. We delight in watching them as they search for a discreet nesting spot and, eventually, take turns nurturing the eggs.

And then, occasionally, when a natural predator snatches their eggs just as they're ready to hatch or a manmade water vehicle runs over the just-hatched, we watch them go through the process all over again.

We know we can't control a hungry raccoon, holiday enthusiasts, or any other Land of Ten Thousand Lakes activity, including the occasional thwacker. After all, this is not *On Golden Pond.* Though this is just the way of life in the modern loon world, we do feel, as co-inhabitants of this lake, some responsibility for their safety. So, once in a while, we get vocal.

Despite our worries, on any given evening, the peepers still peep, the crickets still crick and the loons still party just before dawn.

Scallop Stuffed Mushrooms

Mix together:
2 T olive oil
2 cloves minced garlic
1 t. lemon juice
¼ t. salt

Add, tossing gently:
12 stuffing mushrooms
with stems and gills removed
Let sit while preparing scallops.

Mix together:
4 T melted butter
1 T lemon juice
1 t. unsalted lemon pepper
2 T chopped fresh parsley or 1 T dried
2 T chopped fresh chives or 1 T dried

Add, tossing gently:
12 small scallops
or
6 large scallops sliced in half.

Place the mushrooms on baking pan.
Put scallop in each one.

Bake at 450° 8-10 minutes
or until scallop is thoroughly cooked (140°).
A great appetizer or first course for 4 or 6.

Here's to Adrenaline!

L iability. Friends, family and neighbors cautioned me about potential liability should an accident happen on the swimming raft I had anchored out in the lake in plain view from my deck. While nice that I could easily watch neighborhood kids and my own grandchildren having fun, the raft was also easily accessible and inviting to anyone at the public access.

I have to admit, because it was within an easy swim from the access, some probably did think it was "public." I considered pulling it in during the week when I was at work, but the two concrete blocks used as anchors—after being lodged in the muck—were impossible for me to pull up alone.

I thought about writing up a waiver—you know, like the ones you sign at the gym or when you register for an aerobics class—and having the parents of all the children in the neighborhood sign one before their kids would be allowed to use the raft. However, after years of working in legal offices, I also knew those waivers, in the event of a lawsuit, wouldn't hold up in court.

So, while crossing my fingers that no one got hurt, I resolved to just enjoy the kids enjoying it—my grandchildren, nieces, nephews and their young friends, right along with the neighborhood kids.

Halfway through the summer, my youngest granddaughter, the most enthusiastic swimmer of all, visited for the weekend. That Saturday was the first of the season when water and air temps made it possible to comfortably stay wet all afternoon. I sat on the edge of my dock, paddleboat handy—just in case—and watched her and my neighbor's young daughter jump, screech and swim out at the raft. All afternoon.

A few boys—brothers I vaguely remembered from the next road over—appeared at the access and soon joined the girls. Extra giggles all around increased the entertainment value from my seat. Then things changed. After a couple of debatable slang words, one of the boys let the F-bomb, along with a couple other unmentionables, fly. And as the other two boys, in return, flung back a stream of cuss words, I wondered how they could use every rotten word I'd ever heard all in one sentence and have it make sense.

I've never been one to unnecessarily yell across the water from shore, probably because over the years, I've heard too much yelling from the access. I resisted the urge to do so now. Instead, in no time flat, I jumped in the paddleboat and headed for the raft.

"Boys," I said in the calmest, quietest voice I could manage, "you are certainly welcome to swim and play off this raft, but that sort of language is not tolerable within my earshot, especially when my granddaughter is also here within earshot."

They didn't get a chance to respond before we all heard a woman yelling from the shore of the public access. One hand on one hefty hip and the other pumping in the air, she had everyone's attention. "You sons of #*%!^ better get your skinny little <*)# ! over here before I come out there and beat you so #!^<^%! blue that you won't be able to utter a #!*^%! word out of your !#^%*-%^#!*>ing mouths for a #!%^*>! month!"

She scared the living daylights out of me. I didn't know whether to shoo the boys off the raft or—if this was what they lived with—give them hugs and vow to show them a better way of communicating. I didn't get a chance to do either. The boys were off and swimming toward shore before the girls and I had the presence of mind to shut our hanging-open mouths.

The next morning, my granddaughter and I brought our breakfasts—hers microwaved oatmeal, mine a big mug of coffee—out on the deck. It was quiet, especially peaceful, for a summer Sunday morning. We knew enough to relish it until the access woke up. The low morning sun warmed our faces and our hearts as we chatted about the activities planned for the day. As usual, she was happily anticipating meeting her neighborhood girlfriend out on the raft. Looking at her young slender body, I wondered where she was hiding her fins.

All of a sudden—way too early for a Sunday morning—whoops and hollers traveled across the water and barged in on our serenity. *The brothers.* I have nothing against whoops and hollers, but once they were well into raft rough-housing, the less-than-desirable language began floating over the water.

I was up and in the paddleboat, again using the in-no-time-flat technique and, also again, trying to maintain a calm mode. I repeated my request of the day before. "Boys, I'm glad you're enjoying swimming out here, but my granddaughter and I are trying to enjoy a peaceful morning on the deck, which I might add is within earshot of your cussin'. If you want to keep the privilege of using this raft, you will have to forego the crappy language." I didn't wait for a rebuttal before turning the paddleboat toward shore and double-timing back in.

The "peace" lasted half an hour. Back in the paddleboat, I again pedaled out to the raft. "That's it, guys." I pointed toward the access. "Go." They went. I pedaled hard enough back to my dock that I could only hear every other word of what came out of their mouths as they swam back to shore. Every other word was more than enough to justify my banning them from the raft.

After lunch, my granddaughter and her friend had the raft to themselves. While watching them from the end of my dock, feet hanging in the water, I was relieved there was no sign of the boys. The afternoon was perfectly peaceful and, reluctantly, I returned my charge to her folks early that evening and drove back home to get ready for another work week.

Upon my arrival home, I heard splashing and some of those familiar whoops and hollers before I even stepped out of the garage. And then I heard the other stuff. Against my own advocate-of-quiet-lake-life rules, I marched around the house to the deck and, arm pointing to the access, yelled. "Go. Outa here." I'm sure everyone around the whole lake heard me. They went.

Obviously not becoming bosom buddies with either these boys or their mother, I began worrying for the first time about my liability in the event of a mishap. *Not* for the first time, I wished I could pull those anchors up myself and get the raft in to shore for the week while I was at work and not able to raft-sit.

Instead, after crossing my fingers all day Monday that I wouldn't come home to a summons tacked to the back door, I detoured to the local hardware store. Once home and changed, I grabbed my handy-dandy staple gun, took the paddleboat out to the raft and attached "No Trespassing" signs to two sides of it and "Private Property" signs to the other two sides.

Pleased with myself, I paddled back in, put the staple gun away, took a salad to the deck and enjoyed a quiet, uneventful evening.

The next night I came home to a southeasterly wind, which generally blows any debris from the lake up on my shore. Usually, the debris consists of leaves and branches or, occasionally, a dead fish. This night, the debris included scraps of "No Trespassing" and "Private Property" signs. Instead of another peaceful evening on the deck, I got back in the car and made a beeline for the hardware store.

Just before dark—mosquitoes out in full force—I triple-stapled new signs to the raft and high-pedaled it through buzzing swarms of what has been referred to as the "state bird" to get back to the dock before being eaten alive. I hadn't even had my own dinner! Well past supper-on-the-deck time, I ate my salad on the couch to a *Diagnosis Murder* rerun.

When the ripped-off-signs scene replayed the next night, I was riled. I tried to remember some of the phrases I heard from those boys and their mother. *Hey, there's a time and a place . . .*

I didn't even change clothes before I literally leaped in the paddleboat and shoved off. High heels pumping, silk shirt soaking up sweat, I was on it! I arrived at the raft in record time, hooked up the paddle boat to the eyelet embedded in one corner intended for such a purpose and hopped out onto the top of it.

Giving a fleeting thought to what might happen to my six-dollar pantyhose, I hiked up my skirt and kneeled down on the now-well-worn green carpet and leaned over the edge where one of the anchors was attached. I grabbed the chain leading to a concrete block—the same concrete block sunk in the muck at the bottom of the lake I could never budge—and pulled it up, muck and all, and plopped it on the top of the raft.

Without blinking an eye, I pulled up the second block and plopped it on the back of the paddle boat. Just for a moment, I wondered if this might be the optimum opportunity to belt out "I Am Woman," but I still had work to do.

Back in the paddleboat, I nearly effortlessly towed the raft back to shore and tossed—really!—those blocks onto the shore in order to keep the raft from floating away. *Whew!*

Finally settled on the deck, pantyhose ripped, skirt full of bottom-of-the-lake muck and sweat still running from my temples down to the small of my back, I sacrificed my salad for a beer and toasted the lake . . .

. . . and adrenaline!

Maybe?

She fished. **He fished.** We watched the couple for years—
my husband and I. They would put their canoe in at the
public access and never go any farther than where we
would have to keep our voices low, as we talked on the deck, for
fear of disturbing their serenity. Or scaring away their fish.

Most days, from ice-out to ice-in, they anchored out within
earshot. Appearing as if they were half-way in their lives from
most folks' first job and retirement, we wondered if they even had
jobs. Regular jobs, that is. Could be the fish they gathered might
be a good portion of their diet, lessening the need to earn much
for groceries. Or maybe they sold them. Or . . . Or . . . We hadn't
a clue.

A part of us envied they had the time to hang out on the lake
most of every day. A part of us envied they obviously enjoyed
each other's company enough to hang out together in such close
quarters for most of every day. We also appreciated the fact that

they didn't have the need for an environmentally unfriendly, noisy, gas-guzzling marine vehicle.

We were so in awe of the tranquil routine they seemed so content with that we never even lifted a hand in a hello, as if it might break the spell. One day, once again appreciating their enjoyment of the lake and all it had to offer, we eyed our neglected canoe nestled in the weeds just off shore. We couldn't resist. We dug around in the garage for life jackets and—saying a silent "thank you" for the nudge—went for a cruise ourselves.

~~~

He was tan. She was tan. Each day, even if it were a sweatshirt day for us, she unfailingly showed up in her skimpy black bikini. Her blonde hair tied back in a pink paisley bandana assured her face would catch every ray the sun might have to offer.

He wore shorts—also skimpy. Bare-chested. No hat. Not much hair.

By midsummer, when a pop-up thermometer, akin to those implanted in a Jenny-O turkey, would have deemed them "done," I resisted the urge to share with them our recent experiences with basal cell carcinomas. Most likely launched at about their age, there's nothing like the permanent dent on my nose or the 18-

stitch scar on my hubby's to remind us that Mr. Sun's rays are insidiously powerful.

~~~

She smoked. He smoked. Never did we see them without a cigarette between two fingers or, in the event of pulling up a fish, dangling from between their lips. We wondered which would catch up to them first—the effects of their sun habit or their nicotine habit.

A few years ago, I watched my dad die from the consequences of smoking. Though he had quit several years before, it caught up to him and, within a few agonizing months, cancer had spread throughout his body and took him from us.

Oh, it was from smoking, all right. My dad, not a sick day in his life and wondering what would have caused his demise, asked the oncologist straight out if it might have had something to do with his smoking for 50 years before he quit. Within a heartbeat, the cancer expert said he had never seen cancer of this rampant sort in anyone who had never smoked.

I bit my tongue of the urge to warn this couple, who still had the opportunity to quit years before my dad did and avoid the same happening to them. Then, I thought, *Who in their 40s worries about what might happen in their 70s?* Only those, I guessed—like me—who in their 40s watched their dad, in his 70s, die.

As a sooner challenge, I wondered how long they would have the lung power to pull in a big one.

~~~

No gas? No time? One year—the fifth I think—early in spring as usual, we watched them launch—not their canoe—a fishing boat! Complete with a real motor! The kind that takes gas! And makes noise! Our impressions of this seemingly environmentally conscious couple took a dive.

Surprisingly, with a real boat and motor, in that fifth year, they didn't come out as often. When they did, they never went any farther out on the lake with their new gas-powered marine vehicle than they did with their paddle-powered vehicle.

Maybe it just wasn't as much fun hauling that boat around on a trailer instead of throwing the canoe in the bed of their truck and then easily in and out of the lake. Or maybe the gas cost more than what the fish saved on their grocery bill. Maybe they got real jobs and didn't have time—like the rest of the world!

We speculated enough that we almost believed we knew them and that our made-up stories might be true. We played with ideas for their names.

When I suggested "George" for him, my husband grimaced. "How many guys born in the '70s," he asked, "were named George?"

Then, when he decided she could easily be an "Angeline," I wondered just how much he *did* enjoy her tan, bikini-clad body.

That aside, we missed their regular visits to our lake. One of their last trips out for the season, when they were a little closer to our deck than usual, we waved.

They waved back.

~~~

Maybe? Maybe not? The next season, spurred by our friendly waves at the end of the last year's season, we wondered if we might see them more often. Actually, we hoped.

And, actually, we didn't see them at all. We ran through all the possible scenarios. No gas money? Real jobs? Skin cancer? Lung cancer?

Maybe we shouldn't have waved . . .

That year, about the time the pop-up thermometer would have popped had they been on the lake, my husband turned from the sun-sparkled water to me.

"Maybe," he said, "they caught all the fish."

Fish for Lunch?

Sirens. It was almost noon on Friday when we heard them. I had my nose to the screen of my computer, my fingers wondering what to do on the keyboard in time for my Monday morning writers group.

I smelled the lilies outside my open office window and wondered if life could get any better. I saw my hubby tending to his latest yard project—something to do with rocks.

It was a sunny, gorgeous, perfect July lake day. Eighty degrees. So far. We were looking forward to happy hour. Later. On the deck. As usual.

And then came the sirens. While we have our favorite and not-so-favorite access sounds drifting over to us as we are enjoying our quiet, comfy, lake life—much of it on the deck— one sound we can do without is sirens.

~~~

Earlier that morning, coffee cups in hand, the sun just beginning to sparkle the lake, we watched a couple of old-timer fishermen regulars launch their old-time red Lund with its two cracked red vinyl fisher chairs, out from the access.

As usual, one of them wore a faded, but nicely fitted, perfectly creased pair of blue cotton pants with a blue plaid tucked-in shirt, topped off with an Indiana Jones style hat on his head. The other wore—also as usual—baggy shorts, slouchy white socks showing off his boney legs, an oversized, not-tucked-in, dingy white T-shirt showing off his also-oversized belly, topped off with a Minnesota Twins baseball cap.

While I wondered how these two ever got together, I envied a lifestyle allowing two oldsters in opposite fashion garb to comfortably spend the first half of each day with their lines in the water, watching the day come alive. Not to mention taking their catch home for lunch.

~~~

I had already noticed, before the sirens, during trips between my office and the coffee pot, that old Lund sitting on the access shore for longer than it generally took them to hook it up and be on their way. But I hadn't seen old-timer T-Shirt or old-timer Jones.

We don't hear many sirens here, miles away from any town. And then I realized they were coming from our own road. That doesn't happen often either, here on our measly mile-long dead-end road.

The last time we heard sirens on our road, a medicopter accompanied them. Instinctively, I listened for the whirr of a helicopter.

Sirens are bad enough, but the number one noise no one needs to hear anywhere, including the public access, is a medicopter trying to find a place to land. As this public access barely has room for three vehicles with attached boat trailers, there is definitely not room for a helicopter.

~~~

My mind went back. To two years before. To another hot, humid, Minnesota July day—the kind where we have to stay in the lake to keep cool—to that last time we heard sirens. And then the helicopter.

A "medicopter," we realized, once we could see it. We watched it hover over the too-small access and then over our too-small yard before finally finding enough open space across the road to put down.

By then, emergency vehicles of all sizes, shapes and sirens had filled the road, which eventually closed to even the locals. The only other vehicle allowed to get through was the one carrying a motorized rubber raft, divers and all the paraphernalia that goes along with that.

Though we didn't know yet exactly what happened where, we had a clue. The to-whom part didn't matter. Our hearts sank, our stomachs turned and our skin grew clammy. And we waited.

I'd like to say this story had a happy ending. Alas, that wasn't the case. We lost a friend that day. There would be no more Bloody Mary happy hours on the pontoon with Gary.

Needless to say, sirens on our road give us the shivers.

~~~

Back in the present, I dared to again look at the access. The one ambulance and one sheriff's car were gone. On this day, I was relieved no medicopter or divers had made an appearance.

Though the lake still sparkled, I didn't see old-timer T-shirt. Just old-timer Jones had re-appeared. He put their usual bucket of fish into the bed of the pickup and slowly, alone, did what they usually did together to pull the Lund out of the lake and went on his way.

I glanced through the open window at the kitchen clock. *Still time,* I thought, *for them to have a late lunch of freshly caught sunnies.*

I'll never know if they had time. Ever . . .

Bloody Mary

In honor of Gary
&
our favorite old-timers

Pour 1 ½ shots vodka
over glassful of ice.

Add:
¼ t. Worcestershire sauce
¼ t. Tabasco sauce
¼ t. lemon juice
sprinkle of celery salt
freshly ground pepper

Fill glass with V-8 veggie juice & stir.
Garnish with slice of lemon
& a short bamboo skewer filled with Gedney Zingers.

Cheers!

The Thrill of the Nest

I ce-out was slow to come this year, here in the Land of Ten Thousand Lakes. Day after day, we watched loons fly in from warmer places looking for enough open water to land. This lake did not yet have it. They would circle overhead a few times, teasing us with their oh-so-familiar call, and then move on. After a few weeks, we worried that maybe, this year, we wouldn't have loons at all.

It is such a thrill every spring when a pair lands on our lake. Officially named the Common Loon, they also have the honor of being the Minnesota State Bird. Needless to say, we are partial to these diving, wailing wonders.

A few folks around the lake are certain the same pair returns every year to the same nesting site, as if they come back because they like us. However, according to experts, all loons know the best location for a nest and that's why one pair might pick the same place as another previously did—not because the landowners near the nest are their best friends.

In addition, loons don't always mate for life or a male might do away with another male in order to take over both his mate and their nest, so it's nearly impossible to be sure the same loon couple returns or even stays together for the season.

Either way, we all like to think we have something to do with their nesting choice. But this year, as pair after pair passed us by, we wondered if we had lost our touch in attracting them. We kept our hopes up though, because in the 20 years I've been here—and nearly 40 for my neighbors—there hasn't been a single year without a successful nesting experience.

Finally, a pair of loons graced us with their presence. While we don't always know the exact spot they choose for nesting or the exact day gestation begins, we do have a clue. Because they take turns tending the nest, as soon as we don't see  them together on the lake anymore, we get out our calendars. We start counting off the 28 days it takes until we see them back out together with a little ball of fluff riding on mama's or papa's back.

Though it was the talk of the lake for the next several weeks, we didn't all agree on the actual conception day. One self-proclaimed expert on loons' mating habits is sure a particular male's yodel—usually in the wee hours of the morning—is the announcement of a successful coupling. Another so-called authority identifies the same by the less-intense intimate hoots shared only between mates or special friends.

No matter the details, we all shared the thrill of anticipating the arrival of a new little one in our neighborhood. However, within a day or two of that circled date on our calendars, the two adult loons were back out on the lake together without the expected little passenger.

Having previously gone through failed nesting experiences, we weren't too worried. It was only mid-June, after all. They had plenty of time to try again. In the past, a second try in a different location always produced a chick. Sure enough, a week later a new nest was spotted on the other side of the lake. Hopes remained high.

A successful nesting is the highlight of every summer. Our entertainment for the rest of the season involves watching the parents feeding small fish to their baby and then teaching it how to dive for food and then finally to fly.

As for my hubby and me, we are fortunate to live close to shallow waters containing smaller fish—good training ground. We don't miss much.

Alas, after another 28 days, this pair of seemingly devoted loons was back out on the lake, still no baby to be seen.

As with the first attempt, no one knows why. Predator? Unusually high lake level? Excessive boat traffic? Poor parenting skills? The only thing we knew for sure was that it was too late in the season for them to try a third time.

While this might be a first for this lake, it may not be the last. You see, many of our Minnesota loons head to the Gulf of Mexico, just off the Louisiana shore, for the winter. As expected, the massive oil spill in the spring of this year is affecting wildlife of all species. Though the verdict is still out, there is a chance some of our precious state birds will not make it back up north next year.

Thus, we may not have even the thrill of the nest, let alone the thrill of watching a chick grow up right out our front door.

Poop Happens

When I first moved here, I didn't have a clue how the bodily functions of a well-known poultry species—which happened to be making this lake their home—would affect my life.

Keep in mind, please, that I don't even eat poultry. Not chicken, turkey, quail, pigeon, dove, duck, partridge or pheasant. And most certainly not goose.

At first, I thought the little goose families were so cute! I couldn't resist taking pictures of them nibbling on the wild rice and tasty weeds right off my deck in this also-cute little lake. That was in the earlier part of the summer season.

By mid-summer, I learned that these little darlings eat everything along the shoreline and from any yard they can possibly waddle onto. And, alas, they excrete it all in the same area in which they dine. This makes for challenging, slimy, smelly strolls around the yard with the grandchildren.

Geese aren't just messy creatures. They are also noisy. Quite the ruckus is made when folks all around the lake shoo dozens of them off their lawns several times a day—and sometimes during the night. The resulting honking and flapping, as the younger ones wave wings that don't yet get them off the ground while shuffling back to the water, is deafening. The shuffling ends with a group splash when they reach the edge of the lake.

In long discussions over campfires or out on the lake with neighbors, we've shared potential remedies. Like spraying grape Kool-Aid on the ground where the geese are most likely to hang out. Evidently, the grape flavoring in Kool-aid is methyl-anthranilate—the main ingredient also in some commercial deterrents—which serves as a sort of tear gas to the geese.

However, from experience, we now know that dew or rain quickly dilutes the fruity mixture, making this an everyday task. Never mind the sweetness attracting other pests. Trading poop for bee stings is an alternative to be carefully considered.

Scattering mothballs around the yard has also been suggested. A quick web search tells us this napthalene product is toxic, not only to moths, but soil, people, pets and wildlife. While the geese can be pesky, we're not quite ready to do them—and everything else—in.

One neighbor with small children who play in the sand near the lake put up a two-foot-high green plastic fence along the shoreline—which doesn't do much for the landscaping—in the hopes it will keep the winged families off the beach. It works only until the goslings learn to fly over it. Multi-colored miniature shovels, intended to be used by toddlers to fill matching pails with sand, end up as pooper scoopers.

Another neighbor strings old CDs across the lakeside of their lot. From our deck, we enjoy the playfulness of the sun-induced rainbow twinkles, but by the time the baby geese can fly over the little green fence, they have no trouble making it over the string of CDs either.

As their flying skills further improve, they can finally get up onto docks and swimming rafts, forcing human lake dwellers to scramble for more elaborate feathered-friend deterrents.

A weekender neighbor attaches colorful helium-filled balloons to his dock. When the breeze bats them around, the geese are supposed to think they're predators. And every Friday when he comes for a nice country lake weekend, he has to first clean off the dock.

Other docks sport scarecrows, rubber snakes or fake foxes. The geese have made friends with them all.

A barking dog charging a gaggle is an extremely effective deterrent. That is, if one wants to stay outdoors all day—and night—in order to sic Rover on the winged creatures. This method backfired on one neighbor's elderly dog when the geese turned on her. One goose-nip and Ginger, tail between her legs, hightailed it back home. And that's where she stays.

Another neighbor installed motion lights near the part of his lawn the geese frequented. Besides the lights waking us up every time a rabbit, raccoon, dog or cat darted by, all they did was make it easier for the poopers to find their way in the dark to the tastiest part of the yard.

My hubby and I have found the answer. Two answers! One for the yard and another for the dock!

Keeping the geese out of our yard takes absolutely no effort. We simply let our shoreline go back to its native state, which makes it a natural goose buffer. It's too much work for them to navigate through the Swamp Milkweed, Blue Vervain, Joe Pye and Boneset to get to the edible stuff. As a side benefit, we get to enjoy the butterflies, dragonflies and hummingbirds that frequent the flowery vegetation.

And, as expected, once the little ones start flying, they have no trouble getting up on our dock. Our goose-defying dock trick? Pinwheels!

We drilled several small holes all over the dock, and each year we insert into them sparkly, metallic, wind-operated pinwheels. Lots of them! And it works!

Side benefit? Sparkles happen . . .

Summer's End

It's the last weekend in August. Marigolds out on the deck are hanging in there. Black-eyed Susans along the shore are at their blossoming best. Monarchs and dragonflies are anticipating a long flight south.

There's just enough of a breeze to barely rustle the leaves. Just enough to put my hubby to sleep on this warm, almost-autumn afternoon, as we sit in the same plastic deck chairs where we shared so many toasts over the summer.

The access is quiet. So is the lake. The geese are gone. I consider taking in the pinwheels we attached helter skelter all over the dock that did a pretty good job of keeping them off. But I've grown accustomed to their sparkly playfulness. Maybe next week. Or the week after.

I also consider putting away the lake toys and the big red and purple plastic slide at water's edge, left over from last week's annual summer family get-together. Not ready yet to dismiss the memories of children laughing and splashing, I instead dismiss the task.

As I mindlessly pinch off a few dead marigold heads, I notice the hummingbird feeder hanging next to the remaining sunshine-colored blossoms, again, doesn't need filling. While we enjoyed the antics this morning of a few of our tiny feathered friends, just passing through, loading up on sugar water to get them to the next stop on their annual trip south, it is quiet now.

Beyond the deck, the lake is curiously void of any marine vehicle that goes fast and makes noise. Even the popular sport of "tubing" has slowed to few-and-far-between, now that kids are getting ready to go back to school. We don't mind.

The most activity going on here is chipmunks scouring for acorns to stash away for winter. Watching them scamper from one herb pot on the deck to another—nibbling scruffy basil, rosemary and thyme leaves, and merely sniffing the fallen dill and coriander seeds—I wonder if they might be gourmet munks.

Though lake activities have been our summer entertainment, more or less, this short time between warm wildness and the onset of leaf blowers—snowmobiles soon after—is a welcome respite.

While we relish our last few 'toon rides on the lake we now have all to ourselves during these last few weeks of summer, I have one lament. I doubt the last of my tomatoes will have enough time, heat and sun to ripen. Green tomato salsa is in the near future. Like most years.

That's summer's end here in this Land of Ten Thousand Lakes.

Green Tomato Salsa

Mix together:
1 ½ C. chopped green tomatoes
½ C. chopped red tomatoes
1 heaping T chopped onion
1 heaping T chopped fresh or 2 t. dried cilantro
1 T minced jalapeño
1 minced garlic clove
1 t. olive oil
¼ t. salt
several grinds black pepper

Refrigerate at least an hour.
Overnight is best.
Stir before serving.
Serve with corn tortilla chips.
Makes 2 cups

Thunk Season

It happens every year. And every year it seems to happen sooner than the year before. Yesterday, while puttering in the yard, a *thunk* on my right shoulder gave me the first clue.

I tried to ignore it, telling myself that, not even September yet, it was much too early for *thunks*. But, that night, as I tried to sleep to the *thunk thunk thunks* on my roof, I knew it was here. Acorn season a/k/a *thunk season*.

The roof concert is like a decrescendo. After hitting our slanted roof at lightning speed—*whop!*—the acorn bounces downward several times—*thunk thunk thunk thunk thunk*—makes its grand finale *thunk* in our rain gutter and then performs its encore bounce up and out and onto the ground.

At times, while relaxing in the comfort of our oversized cushy living room furniture, when an acorn hits our stove pipe, it sounds like a shot. A gunshot! We are nearly shot out of our chairs and heading for cover before we recognize the familiar *thunk*.

I can live with *thunk* season, as long as when I go to bed at night I remember to take advantage of my stash of ear plugs and turn on my white noise machine. My hubby, bless his soul, sleeps through it all. Not fair.

Some *thunk* seasons are more plentiful than others. One year the massive amounts of acorns were unusually pretty—as if they had taken on the elegant grain of an oak board destined for a prime piece of furniture. I was sure I could use them in a crafty venture, so I paid neighborhood children to collect coffee cans full of them for me.

Before the end of *thunk* season that year, I had drilled holes in hundreds of acorns, strung them into several plant hangers and had them suspended, complete with lush plants, from one end of the deck to the other.

By the next spring, the squirrels had scarfed the acorns right off the jute and had a heyday with the contents of several three-pound MJB cans of them I had saved in the garage for future projects. To this day, I still find acorns in boxes, bags and boots, all of which have lost the grain effect I found so appealing.

The worst thing about *thunk* season is that it reminds me of what's coming. Looking across the lake, I see leaves losing their brilliant summer green—another hint of summer's end.

I'd like to go into denial for just a little while longer, but walking down the incline on one side of our house doesn't allow for seasonal escape. Covered with acorns, it's like skiing down a mountain of ball bearings. I wonder if squirrels are laughing at us.

Cooler evenings, spent with neighbors and warm drinks around a campfire popping with oak seeds, also support what we don't want to accept.

Some years ago, I was told by a nursery man that oak trees don't sell well anymore. "Too messy and grow too slow," he said. "What folks want now in their new bare yards are pretty, fast-growing, no-mess trees."

As I look up at the massive arms of the oaks reaching over our home from both sides to meet in the center, it looks as if they are protecting us. It's a comforting feeling.

When I first moved here to my oak haven, I watched my neighbor, at the first *thunk*, frantically rake and burn until the trees and his yard were acorn free. I'm not as fussy about my yard as some, so I just let the chipmunks and squirrels store them up for snacks to get them through the winter. This mindset is a little self-serving as I'm also hopeful a good acorn stash will keep them from getting into other things I have stored in the garage.

On the other hand, chipmunks and squirrels are wiser than we are. As they scurry around the yard hiding as many acorns as they can, I rather doubt they are bemoaning the seasonal situation like the rest of us are.

Though we're a little slow to accept the now-certain end of anything resembling summer, by the time we just can't stand the twenty-four-hour *thunking* any longer, it stops.

And we *thunklessly* slip into a quieter season.

Ain't No Mountain High Enough

I t was one of those years. One of those rare years in Minnesota lake country when the lake is still warm enough in September to jump in. Cool enough, however, that taking the hesitant step-by-step approach borders on torturous. Going for a swim, even in the best of Septembers, requires a one-two-three, no-going-back plunge.

Sitting on our southern-exposed deck late one breezeless afternoon, it felt more like mid-July than mid-September. Finally, the pontoon called my hubby and me to take happy hour out on the lake.

On a whim, we threw on swim clothes—just in case. I grabbed beach towels—just in case. He grabbed a bottle of merlot and a couple of wine glasses—the ones with stems that fit in the cup holders—just in . . . Never mind. No just-in-case there.

We toodled around the entire lake, toasting the sunshine during our first glass, toasting each other on the second, and on the third—well, I forget. Nearing home, we anchored in one of our favorite swimming spots, especially this time of year, as it is not too deep and, thus, warmer than other spots. Being near our home, it is also—as you might imagine—near the public access.

We sprawled out on the seats of the 'toon, our faces—along with the rest of us—trying to soak up enough sun to get us through the inevitable first real fall day that could fall upon us at any time.

Drifting—our minds, not the 'toon—well into la-la land, nothing to do with the wine, I thought I heard sopranic lyrics of a vaguely familiar song.

Nah, just my imagination, I thought. But my mind didn't pay attention to my dismissal. Finally, after old memories of high school gymnasium dances meandered through my brain, it came to me. "Ain't No Mountain High Enough." *Must be a dream.* I rolled over.

About the time I was again well into the drift stage, I heard—in perfect pitch—a similar line, but relating to a valley not being low enough. My eyes popped open.

And then another line, this time something about a river not being deep enough. I wondered the alcohol content of this particular brand of merlot and turned my head to see if my hubby was in the same la-la land I was. Not. He had advanced to snore land.

I sat up in time to hear that, in no uncertain terms, nothing could keep this singer from her lover and realized this melodic voice was coming from the access. Relieved to know this wasn't an alcohol-induced moment, I gave my hubby's shoulder a shake. He rubbed his eyes and sat up just in time to hear her assuring her lover she would always be there for him. No matter what!

We looked at each other and then at the access. A familiar pre-teen gal from down the road stood with a fishing line in the shallow weedy water where catching a sunnie is a given. While reeling the line in and casting it out again, she seemingly effortlessly belted out that not only would she be there for him, she'd hurry!

Diana Ross she wasn't, but it didn't hurt our ears to listen to this child whose parents may not yet have been born when Ross recorded this song. She continued, her voice getting louder, stronger, throatier. Nothing would stop her, she promised, from reaching her heartthrob. Not wind! Not rain! Not cold! Nothing! While we appreciated a well-done blast from the past, we more envied her confidence and freedom to do what obviously felt good without worrying about anyone else. Faded memories of my stomach-turning experiences at about her age—but with extra pounds and zits—giving book reports in English classes made a brief appearance in my mind.

I stood—now zit free and minus most of the extra pounds—and opened the gate on the side of the pontoon. After the final chorus of "Ain't No Mountain High Enough" from our serenader, I turned to my hubby and just before jumping, whispered . . .

"Ain't no lake cold enough . . ."

Listening to the Quiet

One unseasonably warm September Saturday morning, coffee cups refilled one more time, my hubby and I headed for the deck.

We basked in the peacefulness of the lake, as slow to wake up this time of year as we were. Though the morning was too-fast approaching afternoon, we were content to melt into the semi-awake state in which the lake had chosen to linger and listen to the quiet.

Half a cup later, we were startled into alertness by an explosion of noise totally foreign to our spoiled country ears. We looked at each other, dumbfounded, and then toward the disturbance.

There, from an empty boat sitting at the edge of the access, came the play-by-play narrative of a football game—full crackly blast! We soon deduced that the volume was cranked up in order to reach the group of sports fans gathered in a circle of lawn chairs on shore, evidently taking a break from lake activities.

The lake isn't as quiet as it used to be.

My hubby and I have plenty of quiet time during the week so are fairly tolerant of surplus kids, dogs, boats and typical weekend having-fun sounds. In fact, after a long winter of near-solitude, it's often a treat to be exposed to the rest of the world.

On this morning, however, we wondered if these visitors realized that this is home to some of us—and that not everyone is a football fan. And then we wondered if they would do the same at *their* home. However, we knew that after the weekend, we would have the lake to ourselves again, so we resorted to hanging out on the back side of the house, surrounded with noise-subduing oaks, until the end of the game.

The lake isn't as quiet as it used to be.

While, admittedly, we may be more accustomed to complete quiet than most, we are always amazed when fishers or pontooners—professing to love the peace and quiet associated with most of Minnesota's ten thousand lakes—immediately upon launching, turn on their favorite pop radio station. Without fail, the experience of one tune to six advertisements, all surrounded by an obnoxious DJ, accelerates the onset of our happy hour— again, to the back side of the house!

And then, there are cell phones!

On the little country road passing by the access, also within earshot of our deck, teens and adults alike can't seem to go for a walk or a bike ride without a cell to their ear. If they only knew we could hear every word they're saying.

During one recent lakeside happy hour—an especially tranquil one with not even a breeze rustling the leaves—we noticed a man fishing from the shore of the public access. *How nice,* we thought. *A different sort of happy hour than ours, but nonetheless a great way to wind down after a work day.*

When a ringing phone split the silence, we both almost jumped up to answer it until we realized it wasn't ours. Without a breeze to muffle noises, the ringing easily traveled across the waveless water to our ears. Sure enough, the fisherman pulled out his phone and shared his side of a not-so-pleasant conversation with us and whoever else might have been within earshot.

This wasn't the first time we've noticed that a fisherman enjoying the relaxing solitude of the sport and the great outdoors out on the lake ends up on the phone. Since the onset of cell phones, not only can they no longer get away from the rest of the world, we can't get away from *their* world.

The lake isn't as quiet as it used to be.

And because the main road running by the access is now paved—it wasn't when I moved here—it invites midnight dragsters, ATV tricksters and a variety of boat-pulling vehicles. While we are often jarred out of our deck chairs when any one of the above hits the speed bump, it is the waste disposal truck at exactly 4:45 a.m. every Friday that jars us out of our sleep!

The lake isn't as quiet as it used to be.

Yes, things have changed in the 20 years I've lived at the edge of this Land of Ten Thousand Lakes lake. Coming from the Twin Cities, before buying this little cabin, I actually drove out here at midnight once and sneaked around the side of the house to the lakeshore just to make sure there wasn't a factory with a midnight shift on the other side of the lake. There wasn't. There still isn't. *Whew.*

And though on some days, depending on the wind and the season, we can hear the ever-increasingly busy I-94, we can always find a place and time to listen to the quiet.

And we do.

∽

And Now: The Lin & Ken Show!

It's the end of our third pontoon season. After several years of wishing we had a pontoon, a few years ago we finally found a "tiny 'toon" just right for the two of us.

Most of the folks on the tiny lake where we live have 'toons that definitely do not fall within the "tiny" range. In fact, most we watch toodle by us as we sit on the deck are in the "party barge" range. It took us a long time to find our modest fifteen-footer.

Believe it or not, though, I can comfortably seat myself and several of the neighbor gals on the 'toon for an impromptu happy hour. It works. Well, as long as none of us gains a hundred or so pounds.

However, because we also have a tiny yard with no place to store a canoe over the winter, let alone a pontoon or a trailer, we paid much too much the first two seasons to have someone come and get it in the fall and bring it back to us in the spring. It was easy. It was—*gulp*—worth it.

This year, our neighbor graciously offered us his trailer and a spot in his yard where our 'toon could hang out over the winter next to his 'toon. How could we resist?

Thus, finally, after years of watching public access antics from our deck, we had an opportunity to access the public access for ourselves.

And now that we didn't have to depend on making arrangements with someone else to take care of the winter storage issue, we vowed to take advantage of every last possible 'toonin' day. From our deck, sun on our faces, wine glasses in hand, we watched others from around the lake take their pontoons out of the water on 70-plus perfect 'toonin' days. We thought how silly it was to skip any chance of one more wonderful-weather toodlin' day.

Feeling quite clever with our decision to get in every last sunshiny moment on the lake we could, the last hold-out, except for us, actually bowed to us from his deck as we 'tooned by on yet one-more-nice day. We had the lake to ourselves and felt like we were on top of the world—well, at least a little above the rest of the pontoon people who no longer had access to the lake. As long as the forecast showed another 60 or 70 degree day in the near future, we put off taking our 'toon out of the lake. As this year's autumn had been exceptional, we 'tooned well into November. Finally, after a few days of 50-ish degrees—and after another ride or two dressed in winter garb—we decided the time was near. When all of a sudden the temps dipped into the 40s, we wisely—we believed at the time—decided the next sunny windless day we would take it out.

We watched the forecast closely. Living near Clearwater, we debated which forecast might be right—the Twin Cities 50 miles south (his choice) or St. Cloud 15 miles north (my choice)—but in the end it didn't matter. When the rain didn't stop, the temps threatened freezing and the wind was toppling trees, we lowered our expectations of a sunny windless day to maybe just windless. No matter the temp or precipitation factors, the next windless day would be the day we would take out the 'toon.

During the second week of November, that day finally came. It was not a warm day. It was not a dry day. But the wind was on our side for getting the 'toon over to the access. After a couple of hours debating if there might be a slim chance the rain would let up later in the day, but knowing that tomorrow's forecast was worse, we donned the rain gear we had been saving for the overnight camping, hiking trips we never took because, well, we are fair weather sportsters. This day was testing us.

Hubby had the pleasure of driving the trailer over to the access. My job was to drive the 'toon over to the access. After making a circle around the lake to—oh, I don't know, something to do with allowing whatever he put in the motor to run through it—I was to drive the 'toon up onto the trailer that he would have ready and waiting for me.

Now, there are several instances in our married life when I have had to do something either more technical or more physical—or a combination of both—than I am comfortable with. I have finally gotten it through my hubby's head that before I will help him with a challenging techno/physical task, he needs to tell me his plan. Ahead of time.

This was made evident during a recent roof project involving a radio antenna, guy wires, lots of wind and detangling countless of the complicated sailor knots he's quite proud of. Once we were on the roof, me not having a clue what we were going to do until the tasks—in perfect order in his mind—were urgent, this activity was not pretty. But it proved my point.

Linda Marie

So, in keeping with our agreement for him to share his plan, he took time to tell me, while we were still on ground, how far up on the trailer I was to drive the 'toon and how fast and when to cut the engine and when to raise it and maybe a few other details I don't now recall.

After years of listening to other public access users yelling over noisy motors, I was relieved we had a plan and wouldn't be reduced to yelling on-the-spot makeshift directions. However, when the getting-the-'toon-on-the-trailer portion of our plan didn't go completely according to the plan, some verbal communication was required.

He whispered something to me from his place on shore while pointing to the place where the 'toon and the trailer had come together. I pointed to the same area and whispered back. After a few rounds of this method of communication not working for us, I looked around for a potential audience and, thankful nobody else was out enjoying the elements, relayed in a healthy outdoor voice, "According to *your* plan, I *am* exactly as far up on the trailer as I *should* be."

He made a slicing gesture across the front of his neck. I would have preferred a good healthy yell. I stared disbelievingly at my usually mild-mannered, non-violent hubby. I didn't know what to do next. He did the slice thing again. I wanted to cry. I looked around again for an audience and wiped the raindrops—I think they were raindrops—from my eyes. My gaze landed on our deck. I wished I were there.

His real-life yell brought me back to the task at hand. "Cut!" Louder yet, he yelled, "Sweetheart!" He did another slice.

Sweetheart? I thought. *Sweetheart?*

"Cut," he yelled again. And then louder, "Cut the engine!"

He doesn't want to cut my throat? I snapped to and turned the key to the off position.

"Good enough," he whispered. "Let's go." He got back in the car and pulled the trailer, the pontoon and me out of the water. Over the back end of the 'toon, I watched it slide a couple of feet farther down the trailer than was in the plan. I couldn't tell him, without yelling at least, while he was in the car a ways away. So I just crossed my fingers that . . . well, I didn't want to go there.

When he got out to inspect our progress and to tie—with more of those fancy knots—a bright yellow ski rope from the 'toon to the trailer to keep it from sliding off, he noticed the slip. "Oops," he said, holding up the rope, "guess I should have done this first."

I looked around, hoping we didn't have an audience, and slipped into the car.

Though by water, our home is only 50 yards from the access, by land we are half a mile. Coming back home, the last half of that half mile often requires maneuvering vehicles in reverse as there is nowhere along the way to turn around. Oh, and that last stretch is not anything akin to asphalt-paved. In fact, this road can hardly be called a road. It is a gravel thoroughfare on an incline—down heading in and up heading out—with most of the gravel washed out from rains—more of which was happening on this day—leaving behind a rut-filled muddy path more suited to donkeys.

Backing any vehicle down this "road" is always a challenge, but today my hubby had a 20-foot trailer, carrying a pontoon, attached to the back end of his mediocre automobile designed for three mediocre passengers. I wondered if donkeys could be trained to pull a pontoon-loaded trailer—in the rain.

Now, as outlined in the plan, my next task was to guide my hubby and trailer and 'toon backwards down the rutted path and into our neighbor's yard for the winter. This job was another outdoors job. I got out of the car, back into the escalating rain, and stationed myself at the back end of the pontoon/trailer. Because of the distance between us, we realized he could only follow my leads if I yelled. After listening to couples yell at each other for years during times like this at the access, and having already reached our personal yell quota for the day, we established a set of hand signals.

I again looked around for an audience. *None.*

After what seemed like hours of arm signals one way or another as he inched the trailer through and around ruts, I felt like a referee at the Super Bowl. When the pontoon began tipping to one side as the wheels of the trailer threatened to lodge into one of the larger ruts, I wished I had a whistle. Instead, I resorted to yelling. "Stopppppp!"

I looked around for an audience. No one else was nuts enough to be out in this weather. *Whew!*

After several more stops, starts, hand signals and lots of whistle-wishing, the trailer and 'toon landed in a place in the yard we thought we could live with. "Good enough," we agreed. Now all we had to do was winterize the motor, clean out the leaves, and make sure the carpet and everything in, under and around the seats was dry before covering it. A warm sunny day was in order.

It rained for a week. And then it snowed. Finally, the temps climbed to a sweltering 50-something. We took our morning coffee to the deck, thinking it might be a good day to finish our seasonal pontoon tasks. The sky was June-blue and the lake a mirror reflecting the lingering beauty of a few yellow-leaved aspens.

My hubby looked out at the water, behind us at the pontoon, back at the lake and then at me. "Nice day," he said. "Wanna take the 'toon out?"

A Lost Week?

I turned away from the patio door window and put my camera down on the kitchen table next to the binoculars. "My gosh, this has certainly been a lost week," I said, bypassing the multiplying dirty dishes on the counter and, without another look out at the lake, headed for my computer.

My hubby was stunned. "Lost week?"

Just before I rounded the last corner on the path to my little corner of our humble home, I turned to see his grief-stricken face. He looked as if I had dissed the creation of the world.

As his focus turned from me—his crabby wife who hadn't gotten anything done in a week—back to the lake, his expression turned to unbridled joy. "You've gotta see this," he said. He could hardly keep from bouncing with excitement as he waved me back to the window.

I couldn't resist. I started back.

~~~

You see, each year, we are graced with a few trumpeter swans as they make their way north in the spring and, during this season, to wherever they spend the winter. It's always a thrill to see them—the largest native North American water-fowl—swoop in for a graceful landing. If they choose to hang around long enough, it's an extra thrill to watch them lounging or preening at the edge of still-open water where ice has started to form, or bottoms up, nibbling at old water lilies under the surface of the lake.

And honking! Day and night. To the point, at times, of waking us. But the delight in the idea that they choose our lake is always worth a few less winks. We like to think we are special. Like they actually make the conscious decision to hang out with those nice people—us—at the end of the lake next to the public access.

Usually, just a few visit for a few days at most. This year, however, these gorgeous feathered creatures were content to hang out for a full week. And even more astounding was that anywhere from a dozen to a hundred at any one time played, preened and dined along the shore, which happens to be only eight feet from our deck.

At the crack of dawn, whoever was up first—my hubby or me—picked up the binoculars and took inventory. Those binoculars and both of our cameras didn't leave our lakeside kitchen table all week. There was hardly a moment between sunrise and sunset that one lens or another wasn't scoping out the migrating action.

In addition to taking over our days, when nature called me in the middle of the night, I never failed to take a detour past one of the lakeside windows to peer out into the darkness. Several big white fluff balls were usually sound asleep near enough for me to just barely make them out.

On one of those nights I was surprised to see about a hundred swans, in various stages of eating, sleeping and swimming, all lit up. I looked toward the source of the light to see a car parked in the public access with its headlights directed toward this amazing sight.

In contrast, my hubby and I had kept most of our lights—indoors and outdoors—off at night so as not to scare them away. After a whole week of fumbling around in semi-darkness, we realized it didn't make a difference to the swans. And we were happy others, not so fortunate as to live a few feet from the birds' chosen stopover, enjoyed them, too.

Though behind on everything else in our lives, we didn't miss a thing. We spent one afternoon watching a bald eagle—which we usually also appreciate—alternately scoping out the situation from the top of a tree and dive-bombing the swans. Of course, we know predators are a part of the natural world but we didn't want to see what we knew could happen. We hardly breathed until the eagle left without his anticipated dinner. And I have no doubt we left nose prints on the window.

~~~

On the eighth day, my hubby called to me. "Hurry," he said. "They're bobbing!"

Head-bobbing is what we discovered they do while getting ready for take-off. We had watched this phenomenon already many times over the last week and knew the routine, but we still hated to miss it!

I made it to the window in time.

A family of four was heading toward the end of the open sliver of water we had come to call the runway. They shared a few mutual head bobs on the way, as if  discussing the factors that might make this the best time to take off. Or not.

Eventually, they gathered together, turned around to face into the wind, Mom and Dad in front, and the bobbing accelerated. Checking with air traffic control perhaps?

I picked my camera back up, quietly slid open the patio door and stepped out onto the cold, damp deck in my stocking feet. My hubby shook his head, but he was smiling. We went through a lot of socks this week.

Sure enough, the bobbing slowed as they began taxiing down the runway—into the wind, just like a Boeing. Lifting their magnificent wings—the best of them having a span of eight feet or more—and flapping faster and faster, their legs soon lifted enough that they could run across the surface of the water. I clicked and clicked and clicked.

Wings flapping faster still, they managed to lift their bodies up enough that they could pull in their legs. Like landing gear, I thought. Their efforts left us breathless.

My camera dropped to my side as we watched in awe their well-planned ascent. They banked in synchronized form, in harmony with the wind, and gathered speed in order to gain elevation.

My mouth hung open as, by the time they reached the end of the lake, they had elevated only half-way up to the tops of the trees. I needn't have worried. They simply looped around, making another pass down the lake toward us, and continued climbing until they could loop back around once more and make it over the tops of the trees. And then, they were off to warmer waters . . .

We breathed.

By the end of the day—dirty dishes and writing projects still waiting for me—the last of the swans were gone.

"A lost week?"

Only Once

Every year is different here on the lake.

One year we donned shorts and took the paddleboat out after Thanksgiving dinner. Only once. One year we spent the Fourth of July cleaning up trees that had been uprooted during near-tornado storms the day before. Only once. Another year my sisters and I drank frozen daiquiris on Easter while sprawled out on lawn chairs in bikinis working on our tans. Only once.

This year we hadn't had one snowflake by Christmas. And the lake, much to the dismay of ice fishers wanting to take advantage of days off for the holiday, was taking its time freezing.

Heading into another Land of Ten Thousand Lakes winter, we knew it would be a while before frozen-daiquiri weather. We decided not to wait. We made some. And, in our denial of the season to come, took our glasses out to the deck and toasted the not-frozen lake.

And then it happened. We woke up the Saturday after Christmas to a frozen-solid lake. Because we hadn't had winds for a few days, it was also smooth as glass—and just as clear. This was a first. By noon, we couldn't resist and dug out ice skates.

Of course, we've skated on the lake before, but we usually have to battle patches of crusty snow, lumpy frozen-over fishing holes and bumpy snowmobile tracks. Here and there, people occasionally try to maintain an area to skate on, but Mother Nature doesn't usually cooperate.

I've always thought it would be nifty if each resident would just clear a path in front of their house connecting it to the path at the next house, so we could skate all around the lake. Wishful thinking. That's never happened.

But on that Saturday, without any help from my neighbors, I got my wish. My hubby and I laced up our skates and gingerly stepped onto the newly frozen lake. At first, we stayed close to the edges. Because it had frozen so clear, it was difficult to tell how thick the ice was. Little by little, we ventured farther out.

Suddenly, ahead of me, my hubby abruptly stopped and looked down. Half expecting him to go through the ice, I stopped a ways behind him. He motioned for me to come along side of him. I did. Slowly.

"Look," he said. I did. And there we watched fish swimming in the water beneath the ice.

It was magical. In awe, we made our way around the entire lake. By the time we thought we were getting accustomed to the eeriness of the experience, we reached a heap of dried brush on top of the ice just off the shoreline. A muskrat hut.

Though we've seen plenty of these huts, we were curious about what a muskrat house looks like below the water level. We inched closer, bent over and peered through the ice. We both almost jumped straight up when a muskrat scooted out from under us and into his under-ice home. What a sight!

We had barely recovered when we heard voices and, finally, looked up and around us. Lo and behold, dozens of other folks we hadn't seen since boat season ended were out skating, too. And more sat on shores all around the lake lacing up.

Mother Nature gave us two days of this phenomenon before snow and wind took over.

In my 20 years here on the lake, this has happened only once.

Linda Marie

Frozen Lemon Daiquiris

Mix in blender:
1 large can of frozen lemonade
2 lemonade cans of vodka
5 trays ice cubes

May have to blend in stages as all won't fit in blender at once.
(Well, unless you make half a batch. But why?)

Store in covered plastic container in freezer.
Will get slushy but the alcohol keeps it from freezing solid.

Serve in stemmed glass with a short straw.
May garnish with a cherry.

The Serenity of Snow . . .

We woke up this morning to a winter wonderland. While coffee brewed, we gazed in astonishment—as we do each year—at the first snow of the season.

When I turned away to set out cups, my hubby broke out in song. Something about "sleigh bells ringing." And another line I didn't quite catch that ended in asking me if I was "listening." I looked sideways at him, glanced at the clock and then reached up to the top shelf in the cupboard and retrieved the bottle of Kahlúa.

Myself, I didn't hear any sleigh bells, so suffered through his outburst until the last stanza and then couldn't resist joining him. "Thrilling" and "chilling" were the key words here, ending with a walk in "a winter wonderland."

While we do appreciate our own winter wonderland, the Carpenters we are not, and I was glad we were still indoors. And not "chilling."

Winter, here on the lake, is a quiet season. A restful season. A slow season. And, yes, a "thrilling" season.

The magic of waking up in the morning to trees covered with new snow brings about a reverence equal to prayer. And when the white coating is thick enough that we can't get out of the driveway to go to work, we whisper a "thank you" to the snow gods.

On days like this, forcing us to slow down, I often wonder if we, in this climate, should be hibernating and we're just too dumb to know it.

Okay, though we don't have a lot of bears here in the center of the Land of Ten Thousand Lakes, we do have chipmunks. And though they can make a mess out of the garage and scarf all the food intended for our feathered friends, the life of a chipmunk is one to be envied. Just imagine napping through winter, getting up once in a while for a snack and then hitting the snooze button again.

Today happened to be one of those days we are forced to hibernate—at least until the driveway is plowed. As we looked out at the yard in awe of the changes since yesterday, we secretly hoped the 80-something guy up the road who does the plowing for us was having a low-energy day himself.

Taking our Kahlúa-laced coffee to the deck—mostly to warm our hands as we surveyed the snow-covered lake from the one spot under our eaves where we didn't have to wear boots—we marveled at the marshmallow-like surface reminding us of winter fields and lakes in our childhood.

We knew the untouched vastness would only last until any snowmobilers lucky enough not to have to work on a Tuesday quit hitting their own snooze buttons. We clinked cups, toasting the trackless lake while it was still trackless.

Interrupting the silence of the snow, we heard the township's plow on the road running by the public access. Living on an adjacent gravel road, we do not have that service and are grateful for the times the lack of that luxury allows us a day off from work.

Even the access will be taking a break for a while, as that's where most of the snow from the road is piled. There's not much room left for ice-fishers to park and barely enough room for a daring snowmobiler or cross country skier to get to the lake via the access.

Finally, returning inside, we put our empty coffee cups in the sink, turned off the pot and retrieved our Mukluks from the top shelf in the shoe closet. It was time to clean the cobwebs off the snow shovels and brave the drifts we knew would have accumulated on the backyard walks.

The first bend in the walk leading from the house to the garage was a sight to behold. We only wished the grandchildren were here to see how their beloved tire swing looks on a day like this. Drifts of snow stretching across the walk and around the swing made reaching it impossible, while another foot of snow frosted the top of it. But we were on our own today. If we can't get out, no one can get in either.

After the path around the garage was cleared, we decided to take a break on the other swing, designed for adults and strategically placed in the corner of our yard facing west to capture the view of awesome sunsets.

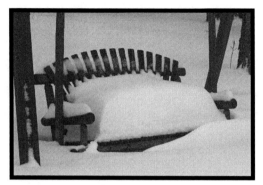

Alas, that too was inaccessible today. And the promise of more snow to come wiped out the possibility of a Kodak sunset later.

We had just finished shoveling the parts of our yard not conducive to plowing and were unlacing our Mukluks inside the back door when the phone rang. I dripped across the floor to answer it.

"So," our 80-something plower said, "do you need to get out today?"

I looked at my hubby, rosy-cheeked from our winter-induced endeavor. I looked out the back window at the snow-covered trees and swings and out the front window at the still-trackless lake.

I opened the fridge. *Yup, salmon in the freezer and broccoli in the crisper.* I glanced up at the wine rack . . .

"No," I said, "we don't have to go anywhere."

Aah, the serenity of snow . . .

Snow Day Salmon with Herb Mustard Glaze

Combine in blender for about 30 seconds:
1 chopped garlic clove
1/2 t. finely chopped fresh rosemary or 1/4 t. dried
1/2 t. finely chopped fresh thyme or 1/4 t. dried
1 T white wine
2 t. extra-virgin olive oil
1 T Dijon mustard
2 t. whole-grain mustard

Transfer to bowl.
Add & stir in:
1 more t. whole-grain mustard.
Set aside.

Spray foil lined pan with oil.
Arrange 4 4-oz. salmon fillets on pan.
Salt & pepper to taste.

Broil a few minutes.
Spread mustard sauce over tops.
Broil until golden brown & 140° in centers.

Serve with lemon wedges & steamed green veggie.
Serves 4

Where's the Evidence?

I don't like to think of myself as a snoopy old busybody, but living within earshot and eyesight of the public access does give me—and my binoculars—an advantage to witnessing various, sometimes questionable, activities. Not that I'm looking for trouble, mind you, but if something just happens to happen at or near the access, well, how can I not take a peek?

Rarely have I seen anything suspicious enough to lure my fingers to dial 911. The non-emergency number listed in the phone book for local authorities usually serves the purpose. Like, when a stripped down boat was left on the shore of the access for days. Turned out to be stolen from another lake and, with anything of value ripped out, was dumped here.

And then there was the gorgeous summer morning when the hummingbirds called me and my coffee to the deck. I glanced over to the access and saw a truck, with no driver, nose down and half sunk into the lake. Imagining a driver passed out at the wheel and slowly sinking further, I figured this was a 911 moment and did my duty. By the time I hung up and turned back to the window, the truck was gone.

Another instance my fingers gave in to dialing 911, I thought for sure a drug deal was under way. The shady-looking characters lurking under the cover of dense brush at the edge of the access, surely up to some kind of no good, were gone by the time the good guys got there.

I generally try to keep my nose out of other people's business. Like when the young teens down the road use the access to test their smoking skills, I don't even consider making a call. It only brings back memories of my friends and me—in our thirteenth summer—learning how to smoke down on the shores of the Mississippi. To this day, none of the six of us has taken up the habit for good. Might have had something to do with experimenting on Chesterfield non-filters because that's what Maggie's folks smoked and she was the best copper in the group. But, that's a story for a different day. Anyway, seeing the kids test their nicotine tolerance doesn't make me dial 911.

One night, however—actually, one morning—in January, I woke up around 3 and noticed a car driving out on the ice, from the access to just beyond my house. With not much else to do at 3 in the a.m., I picked up the binoculars.

I watched this car roll to a stop out in the middle of the lake. I watched two guys open up the trunk. I watched them, by the light of the car's headlights, set up a portable fish house.

Putting up a fish house during the day during a Minnesota winter is no big deal. But in the dark? I watched them haul unidentifiable objects from the trunk into the house and then drive back to the access and off the lake. Though odd, I was accustomed to odd and innocently thought they would be back later in the morning to fish.

Silly me.

They came back, all right—at 3 the next morning. No, I didn't stay up all night waiting for them. I may not be much of an old busybody, but I am old enough that nature calls often. As I passed by the lakeside window, I caught just the faintest movement out on the lake. Sure enough, the same car was headed toward the fish house—this time without the headlights on. Guess they didn't want to scare away the fish . . .

I picked up the binoculars and, following the sounds of cracking ice, watched the vehicle stop at the fish house. The interior car light flickered as both doors opened and a guy got out

each side. Another light came on as they opened the trunk and lifted out more objects I couldn't identify. Bait, perhaps? A deck of cards and some chips? After several trips transferring stuff into the little house, they closed the trunk, disappeared inside the tent-like structure and zipped up the door.

I attended to my own business and went back to bed.

Three hours later, my next trip by the window revealed the car was gone. I vowed to myself to share with my fisher brothers that the fish must be biting well enough in the wee hours to warrant a few hours of missed sleep.

The next night, the whole routine repeated, they were again gone before dawn. And again the next night. And the next . . .

After explaining the scenario to my neighbor during our morning walk, we agreed that it seemed a little fishy. Maybe a

911 call was in order? That night I went to bed with the idea that the next time those guys were safely zipped in, I'd make that call. So, in the wee hours, phone in hand, I looked out the window into the especially dark, moonless night. Nothing. I picked up the binoculars and looked. Nothing. No house. No car. Nothing. Later that morning, my walking friend and I decided to walk on the lake instead of the road. We followed car tracks to where the fish house had been. In the midst of beer cans, matches and remnants of what looked like a rug that had caught on fire, there was a good-sized frozen-over fishing hole. We peered through the ice and saw a bright yellow plastic bottle with big blue lettering, frozen in place, looking mysteriously like what I put in my gas tank when Minnesota temps reach 40 below. I kicked at a small flattened piece of cardboard, which flipped over—the same over-the-counter drug I take for a cold.

During our walk back home, we debated the likelihood that these guys were actually fishing. We decided we'll never know for sure.

But I'll bet the rest of the evidence is at the bottom of the lake.

Crafty Critters Win! Again . . .

"Get outa here!"

This is what I hear, along with a few knocks on the window, from my hubby's office at the other end of the house. Accustomed to these sounds during winter months, I continue my keyboarding tasks in my own end of the house.

And then I hear another. "Get outa here!"

And then I hear the window slam shut.

Whew, I think, *he's getting serious.*

And then another, "Get outa here!"

And another slam.

I don't have to get up to figure out what's going on. I have my own window. I stop typing and look out at the snow-covered yard my hubby has made into a birds' winter-feeding paradise.

Hanging from the roof's gutter just outside my window is a cylinder type feeder that attracts finches and other small birds. A similar one hangs outside my hubby's office window.

In the middle of the yard is a flat style feeder that attracts cardinals. And hanging from two of the big oaks are suet feeders bringing in chicadees, nuthatches and a variety of woodpeckers.

Blue jays make pigs of themselves wherever there's food, while charcoal-colored junkos and one lone female pheasant clean up whatever ends up on the ground.

The "get-outa-here" issue today is the house-type feeder stationed on a pole in the middle of our bird-feeding paradise. A brand new feeder!

For all of my husband's efforts, we don't have as many birds as we used to. You guessed it. Squirrels.

Actually, the reason for the brand-new feeder was because these "medium sized rodents"—according to Wikipedia—trashed the old one.

The Chinese calendar says this is "the year of the rabbit." I'm thinking it should be "the year of the squirrel." Besides eating all the birdseed, their fat furry presence in the birds' dining room scares our feathered friends away.

We've tried everything short of target practice to keep the crafty critters off the bird feeders.

Expert birders suggest switching to safflower seeds—that birds like it but squirrels don't. Sounds like an easy remedy. And they're right—the squirrels stay clear of it. However, I don't know what kind of birds the experts have, but our birds also stay clear.

We've experimented with adding cayenne pepper to the seed—guaranteed to keep the squirrels away while not affecting the birds' appetites. It works! For a while. Not long enough. In the end, the red powdered spice clumps and makes a mess in the feeders. And by then, it doesn't bother the squirrels' taste buds either.

Mom to the rescue! "Oil," she said. "Rub oil on the pole. Makes it too slippery for them to climb up."

Enthusiastically, I relayed the message to Hubby. He reminded me that we had already tried the vegetable oil thing and that when spring came, the blowing-in-the-wind cottonwood fuzzies attached themselves to our oil-coated pole. It all came back to me. Gross. Impossible to clean.

I relayed that back to Mom. "Oh no," she said. "Not vegetable oil. Castor oil!" She explained that after ingesting the oil by licking it off their feet, digestive issues keep them from raiding the feeders. Not wishing to deal with the potential mess in the yard, we decided to file this potential remedy away for possible future use.

By this time, the squirrels had also mastered jumping from a tree to the roof, hopping over the gutter and climbing down the bungee cords attached to both hanging feeders outside our office windows. These plastic feeding tubes were now chewed up enough that seed wouldn't stay in them to even give the birds a chance. Down they came.

They are smart little buggers.

While googling new remedies one day, I ran across a "no-fail" idea utilizing Slinkies to keep the squirrels from climbing up the pole to reach the feeder.

I put "Slinky" on my Walmart list. Remember Slinkies? It sounded like such a crazy—but, to me, sensible—idea that I didn't even tell my hubby before buying one. I relished thoughts of the kudos I would receive when our critter crisis was magically resolved!

Upon returning home on errand day, I proudly presented him with the colorful little box containing the neatly coiled toy we remembered mostly as a tangled ball of metal wires. But we are grownups now—most of the time—and got down to the task at hand.

According to the online directions, we shortened it, fastened it to the bottom of the new feeder and let the springy coils fall partway down around the pole. We imagined a squirrel climbing up the pole on its usual way to dinner, reaching the first coil of the Slinky, grabbing on and slinking to the ground. Anticipating the fun to come, we could hardly contain ourselves.

And then, we waited.

We were not disappointed. The first squirrel, unable to control its curiosity, climbed up the pole, approached the first coil and gingerly touched it with one of its front feet. And then the other. And then, in a shorter version of its usual leap of faith, leaped with both front and back feet a few coils farther up. And— boinnngggg—the Slinky slinked to the ground, squirrel hanging on for dear life. It was already worth the buck-ninety-six sunk into this particular remedy.

We certainly had our laughs over the next few days watching the feeder robbers figure out this new deterrent. And figure-it-out they did. Once they mastered hanging on through the slinks, this so-called remedy simply turned into a convenient little ladder allowing them to easily climb right up to the feeder.

My hubby went back to his tried-and-true squirrel deterrent. "Get outa here!"

Frustrated, he reached into the depths of his memories and remembered seeing a bird feeder designed so when a squirrel jumped on it, its weight would prompt a twirling action, eventually flipping the dizzyingly drunk-like squirrel off it. "If nothing else," he said, "it would be worth a laugh!"

Straight to Amazon.com I went.

We decided $149.99 was not in our bird budget. In hindsight, however, we realized that in addition to feeder replacement costs, we had fed the bottomless beings at least that much worth of seed so far this season.

In desperation, I put out a notice to friends, requesting their tried-and-true squirrel-prevention methods. The only surefire scheme I received from a friend down the road was that when they took down all the bird feeders, they had no more problems with squirrels. *Hmmm . . .*

We weren't quite ready to fold.

Once again, I heard, "Get outa here!" Only this time, instead of yelling through an open window, he ran outdoors without a jacket in zero degrees. *No wonder he can't get rid of that Christmas cough.*

By the following week, the squirrels were accustomed to the yelling. My hubby gave up on the "get outa here" method. The only way we could have gotten them off the feeder was, perhaps, by grabbing their tails and pulling them off.

Not.

I had always fought the idea of those ugly plastic squirrel guards placed around feeder poles. But, thinking of my hubby's health—mentally and physically—I relinquished. Straight to Fleet Farm he went. Before bird dinnertime that day, it was installed. We sat back and watched the squirrels' bafflement at the new baffle.

The baffle bafflement didn't last as long as it took to install the ugly thing. The squirrels immediately figured out that a measly 15-foot flying leap from the nearest tree would land them right on top of the dining hall. A simple acrobatic maneuver then allowed them to access dinner.

They just keep proving what smart little buggers they are. Meanwhile, my hubby resumed the get-outa-heres and is losing his voice.

The next time I looked out my office window, that nice new feeder was no longer atop the pole. We now had no feeders in the entire yard. Guess the neighbor's idea wasn't so unlikely.

Little did we know the critters would provide us with further entertainment. They were so accustomed to jumping to the feeder from their favorite take-off points, they kept jumping to the same

place and, because there was nothing on top of the pole to land on, overshot, and landed on the ground 15 feet the other side, resulting in a furry somersault.

Because of worsening wintry weather, my hubby nursing that darn ol' cough and no effective feeder to refill, we didn't step out of the house for a few days. With streaming movies, a hot tub and a healthy supply of seafood, veggies and wine, we didn't need to.

And I was glad his under-the-weather voice was getting a reprieve.

Finally, in spite of the stay-indoors weather, I decided to walk up the road to the mailbox. I bundled up, stepped out the door and saw where my hubby had deposited that nice new bird feeder. On our back steps. Upside down. Evidently, he must have figured if the squirrels couldn't reach the seed through the usual outlet, the seed and the feeder were safe.

Well, during our winter escape, they had been busy. Managing to chew up a good portion of the wood preventing them from reaching the seed, heaps of woodchips scattered about gave the illusion we lived in a sawmill.

We realized there was nowhere to hide the feeder without inviting seed-loving critters right to it. There had to be a way to keep the munchkins off it. We put our thinking caps back on.

We ruled out spikes sticking out of the feeder so they couldn't comfortably land on it. We couldn't bring ourselves to cutting the trees down so they didn't have a vaulting point. Poison was out of the question—we're not *that* cruel. And we couldn't move the pole the feeder was mounted on, as the ground was frozen.

I had a few other lame ideas, but when I could sense the wheels already turning in my hubby's head, I decided to keep my mouth shut.

Next thing I knew, he was attaching the bird feeder—filled to the brim—back on top of the pole. With adornments! With the new baffle still intact below, he had attached, helter-skelter on the top, the Slinky!

Brilliant! I thought. *How on earth could they jump from the tree and land on the coiled maze?*

As an extra security measure, my soft-hearted naturalist spread peanuts on the ground under the feeder—as a deterring enticement for the squirrels.

This morning, peanuts gone, the squirrels have made their way around the metal coils and are, as usual, scarfing.

The crafty critters win. Again . . .

In My Dreams . . .

'T is winter in Minnesota.
In fact, we've suffered through two months of February frigid and it's not yet February. Thus, the public access is quiet. The lake is quiet. Day and night!

During the day, even die-hard winter enthusiasts aren't taking advantage of the lake. Few fishers are sitting on overturned buckets hoping to hook dinner through a hole in the ice. Snowmobile activity, in spite of this year's surplus of snow, is way down. Kids aren't skating. Toddlers aren't getting their fill of sled rides. Cross country skiers? Zilch.

And during the night? Nothing. When I'm up in the middle of a sleepless night, there's absolutely nothing going on out there to watch, wonder or worry about. No drug deals. No kissing games. No adolescent tobacco testing. No meth labs . . .

All in all, there's just not enough going on in any season to be awake 20 hours out of 24. But this winter, my insomnia took a turn toward torture. I longed for sleep. Deep sleep. Dream sleep. I couldn't remember the last time I dreamed.

After an especially sleep-deficient month, I decided to take action. To be aggressive! To fight! To win! And, hopefully, to sleep!

Knowing exercise is important for optimum sleep, each afternoon, I bundled up against below-zero windchills and went for walks out on the lake. Trudging through thigh-high drifts of snow, I told myself it was, appropriately, good toning for winter thighs. However, my thighs didn't care.

Like, who's gonna see them these days anyway? Finally, the rest of the frozen me didn't care either. *What does it matter when I never peel off any of my customary winter three layers?*

I moved on to the matter of sunlight—or lack thereof—and its effect on sleep. Anyone who has spent any time in Minnesota during a non-summer season knows sunlight is at a premium. I know because I paid quite a premium for my HappyLight®. As light therapy promises to promote good mood and good sleep, I faithfully spend happy hour with my HappyLight while daydreaming of toodling around the summer lake on the pontoon with my hubby. The effect my HappyLight might have on my sleep I haven't yet figured out. But turning it on, basking in its brightness and pretending it's July isn't all bad.

Fun activities are also supposed to help those of us with sleep issues. My hubby and I like to dance which, according to the experts, should have the potential of helping me sleep. Ha! During the summer we can't bring ourselves to leave the lake to hang out in a dark windowless bar, no matter the music, because it's so nice out. Usually, we depend on the rest of the year to catch up on our steps. This year, though, we can't bring ourselves to leave the cozy warmth of the house to go dancing because it's so *not* nice out!

Desperate, I decided to study up on any sleep remedies I hadn't yet tried. Chalking off previously experienced Ambien, Tylenol PM, acupuncture, hypnosis and an assortment of dirty-sock-smelling herbs, my research led me to melatonin. This "naturally occurring hormone" is reported to be "important in the regulation of circadian rhythms" and, in the end, sleep. *Hmmm, sounds good.*

After also learning about the pineal gland and tryptophan and cortisol levels and electromagnetic fields and much much more about whatever the experts say happens to be related to the body's production of melatonin, I had just about made up my mind to give it a shot.

Then I read about studies which reported an increase in vivid dreams when participants regularly took melatonin. And then I read that the vivid dreams were basically vivid *erotic* dreams!

Straight to the local melatonin supplier I went.

Now, because I am generally health conscious, I decided that along with my new venture in healthy sleep habits, I would also try to counteract the winter-blah syndrome, not to mention the few-extra-winter-pounds syndrome, by embarking on a good-old-fashioned calorie-counting regimen.

Though what I really longed for was a jump into a warm sunlit summer lake, I was excited about my renewed health goals. I opened a new document in my trusty word processing program, made a chart, complete with days of the week and spaces for meals, snacks, exercise, water and even wine intake. I was determined to be ruthless! Honest! Non-forgiving! I was gonna beat the sleepless chubby winter blahs!!!

For three weeks I faithfully recorded my caloric intake and physical expenditure. I took my melatonin faithfully. In fact, because the directions on the 2.5 mg. bottle said to take it before going to sleep and, because I needed to go to sleep more than once during a night, I took a dose before going to bed and again every time I awoke. I was gonna do this right!

A new issue emerged. Every time I woke up I was starving. I started wishing those little white tablets were encased in a grilled cheese sandwich or an "everything" pizza or anything equally scrumptious that I could sneak by my one-thousand-calorie daily allotment.

To take my mind off my complaining belly during awake moments in the night, I'd stroll by the window overlooking the access which—thanks to the township plow—had been transformed into a snow mountain. And then I'd look at the moon-scattered sparkles across the snow-covered winter lake and try to imagine how it would look in a few months. When the moon started looking like a scoop of ice cream and the sparkles like an overdose of sugary sprinkles falling on the lake, I gave up my midnight strolls through the house.

Finally, with the help of multiple doses of melatonin, I slept between the hunger pains. I looked forward to those vivid erotic dreams. I waited for those vivid erotic dreams. For three more weeks, I recorded my calories, listened to my stomach growl, popped the melatonin and slept.

And, finally, I dreamed. Though not what I had anticipated, it was a delicious dream.

I was gorging on chocolate. Dark, luscious, wicked chocolate. It slipped too easily, too dreamily, down my throat and left me wanting for more. I couldn't remember the last time I had a hunk of anything remotely related to fermented cacao beans.

Best of all, I was washing the chocolate down with beer. Beer? After my switch a few years ago to the grape-based beverage typically served in a glass with a stem, I had nearly forgotten the rich, nutty, sweet taste of a roasted-barley brew. I could almost feel the foam on my upper lip, the bubbles tickling my nose . . .

The dream was certainly vivid. But, erotic?

The next night my dreams gave me the task of figuring out how to imbed hunks of bananas in marshmallows and coat the whole works in melted Baby Ruth bars. Try as I might, my sleepy brain couldn't figure out how to do that.

Finally, a "hunk" of the male persuasion appeared on the perimeter of my dream. Hard hat, big bright yellow all-weather jacket, sturdy boots. Dark golden, poreless skin, a scrumptious 3 a.m. shadow and wild wavy hair—the same color as his skin—escaping his hat and begging to be touched.

Hmm. A construction worker straight out of a Greek Harlequin?

I remembered, even in my sleep, reading a story long ago about a Maytag repairman coming to the door of a scantily clad housewife, home alone. I had my hopes up. Wondering if this was an invitation to "erotic," I invited the hard-hat guy into my dream.

He stepped into my dream kitchen and immediately took charge of the situation. *Just like in the romance novels,* I thought.

By the time he finished showing me exactly how to layer bananas, marshmallows and melted candy bars on tortillas to make what looked suspiciously like an "everything" pizza, I was more hungry than, well, you know . . .

The next morning I fired up the Internet and went back to those studies I found in my original research on melatonin and discovered the problem. The studies were made only on men!

Duh. They get vivid erotic; I get vivid junk food!

After another week of pointless calorie-counting and an abundance of vivid food dreams—complete with vivid guilt—I started wondering if I was eating my dreams.

Finally, after discussing with my hubby one evening about getting our seven-year-old grandson a set of his favorite books for his birthday, I dreamed of something besides food.

Yes!

Are vivid "Captain Underpants" dreams getting closer to vivid erotic?

'Tis winter in Minnesota . . .

Linda Marie

Greek "Everything" Tortilla Pizza

Lightly oil pizza pan.
(Pizza pan with holes works best.)

Cover pan with tortillas of your choice.
Spray tortillas lightly with olive oil.
Smooth minced garlic into oil.

Top with:
coarsely chopped raw shelled shrimp
chopped yellow bell pepper
chopped roasted red bell pepper
chopped sun dried tomatoes
sliced scallions
sliced black olives
oregano
basil
crumbled feta cheese
shredded mozzarella cheese

(Add marshmallows, bananas & candy bars at your own risk.)

Bake at 400° or until tortillas are crispy and cheese is melted.

144

About

Another Angle:
Reflections on the Ordinary

This wonderful little book is chicken soup for weary people.

—Jeanette Blonigen Clancy
Author of *God Is Not Three Guys in the Sky*

Definitely a fun read. Linda Marie makes us stop and look at everyday experiences from a whole new perspective.

—Judy Lindroth Kallestad
Author of *Breaking Tradition: A Great-Granddaughter's Search for Her Swedish Roots*

Reading Linda Marie's 'Another Angle' is like visiting with the kind of friend everyone loves—insightful, quirky, and always entertaining. Pour yourself a cup of your favorite tea and enjoy!

—Eve Wallinga
Author of *Waterfalls of Minnesota's North Shore: A Guide for Hikers, Sightseers, and Romantics*

Linda's writing describes common things uncommonly well.

—Robert Roscoe
Co-Author of *Legacies of Faith*

Linda Marie's writing explores and explains simple life experiences from 'Another Angle,' one that is fresh, innovative, perceptive and just plain fun reading. This is a book well worth picking up for a nice comfortable read on a rainy afternoon—or on a bright sunny day. It will make you smile.

—Marilyn Salzi Brinkman
Author of *Aprons, Flour Sacks and Other Folk Histories*

More About

Tales from the Public Access: A Celebration of Lake Life in the Land of Ten Thousand Lakes

Linda Marie's writing is fun and funny. It deliciously pictures life—both human and animal—on Minnesota lakes. But it also creates scenes that make us pause and ponder, maybe even disturb us. I challenge readers to consume only one vignette at a time. Bet you can't do it.

—Jeanette Blonigen Clancy
Author of *God Is Not Three Guys in the Sky*

A public access is a wonderful thing in the land of ten thousand lakes, especially if you live near enough to participate in its activities. Or, sometimes it's an intrusive thing that keeps you from participating in your own activities. Linda Marie grasps both horns of that dilemma with humor and understanding in a presentation that brings into focus people, their foibles, their successes and flops, as they cope with one of Minnesota's delightful lakes. It's a read that's as pleasant as her lake.

—Jerry Holm
Author of *The Retiree: On to Geezerhood*

Author Linda Marie documents the natural and man-made landscapes with a painter's eye. I know of no other author who writes about the culture surrounding the public access. Many of Marie's pieces also show how environment shapes marriage and other personal relationships. Marie's voice is a welcome addition to the list of Minnesota writers

—William Towner Morgan
Author of *Earth, Wood, Stone: Central Minnesota Lives and Landmarks*